I GAVE IT MY BEST SHOT

by Willie Fordham

The (First-Pitch) Baseball I threw to homeplate prior to the Harrisburg Senators game on July 19, 1994 at Riverside Stadium, Harrisburg, PA

Published by Wordshop Press, 123 Forster Street, Harrisburg, PA 17102.
Phone: 717-233-7611

Text and Cover Design by Signal Graphics Printing
Cover Illustration by James Mackey and Kim Robson

ISBN 0-7596-7816-2
Registration No. TXU761-516

Submitted to the Library of Congress for cataloging in publication data under the title of "I GAVE IT MY BEST SHOT", 3rd ed., by Willie Fordham

About the Author

by Stephen, Daniel and Byron Fordham

Our dad is married to our mom, the former Jessie Caroline Fountain. He was born in Millerstown, Pennsylvania and later lived in Newport, PA. He also resided in Carlisle where he had a distinguished baseball career at Carlisle High School. During his senior year at Carlisle, he had a pitching record of 8 wins and no losses, including a no-hit pitching performance. He served his country during World War II in the U.S. Army, stationed in Germany for the majority of his tour. He earned and received his Bachelor of Science degree from Cheyney State Teacher's College and joined the Alpha Phi Alpha fraternity.

He played professional baseball in the U.S. and Canada. While in Canada he coached the Schwab Pee Wee baseball team, which created a bond and friendship with the players and team sponsor that has lasted over forty-eight years. He returned to Canada (Belleville, Ontario) to attend a reunion of the Schwab Pee Wee baseball team members in 1994, forty-three years after that special summer he coached the team.

In early 1952, he had a tryout with the (Major) National Baseball League Brooklyn Dodgers. During the tryout, he had a chance to meet Brooklyn Dodger favorites Jackie Robinson and Roy Campanella. This tryout would prove to be a major turning point for his future.

He was employed with the federal government from August 1952 through July 1982. He is owner and operator of Greenford TV, which has served the local community through its sales and service operations for the past 36 years. He has received many letters of praise and recognition from prominent local, state, and federal officials for his various accomplishments. He still resides in Harrisburg, Pennsylvania with our mother and is currently employed by the Pennsylvania State Department in their clerical pool. We love them both very much.

Our dad desires to publicly air his life story to inspire others who have come close to stardom and/or success but missed the target. He believes and encourages everyone to keep their eyes on the prize and don't ever give up. Dad knows he has been blessed and looks forward to the future. Hopefully the best is yet to come; but no matter what, **he continues to give it his best shot!**

Dedications

This book of my personal memories is dedicated to my mother **Mrs. Mary Edwards** who departed this life November 18, 1993. She was a loving and caring mom who taught me how to cope with ups and downs in life. She is my hero, my champion.

and to

My wife **Jessie** who has been a pillar of strength, keeping the good ship **"FORDHAM"** on a steady course. Without her inspiration, this book would not have been written.

and to

My three sons, **Stephen**, **Daniel** and **Byron**, who have all grown up to be fine outstanding men. The quality time spent with them was a blessing. They will keep the **Fordham** banner hung high for all to see.

Special Thanks to...

My sister **Mary** and brother **Paul**. They are there when needed.

Family friend **Pam Chavis** and son **Stephen**. They compiled and assembled the mountain of detailed background information related to my various accomplishments. As the direct result of their efforts, numerous letters of public praise for accomplishments (detailed in this book) were received from many prominent professional leaders/ organizations.

Ted Schwab. He provided the tools (bats, gloves, shoes, etc.) needed by the 1951 Schwab Pee Wee baseball team to win, and win they did!

Dick and Judy Hurst. They took time out to host the September 17, 1994 reunion of the 1951 Schwab Pee Wee baseball team members. Superb job! A thrill that will surely last a lifetime.

Bern Sharfman. He provided his professional editorial review of the first draft of this book and pointed out the areas that needed more detailed explanation or clarification.

Doctor Stanley Lewin. He provided professional treatment for my heart ailments. He is a great credit to the medical profession.

Introduction

In order to adequately describe events which shaped my development and philosophy of "giving it my best shot", this autobiography begins by highlighting the early years of my life's journey; a journey which has been filled with much enjoyment and some disappointments. Along the way, I have always taken time to count my blessings. My advice to all, especially young people, is to follow your dreams, never give up, and don't get bogged down in self-pity. Remember the glass of water is half full rather than half empty, and in the arena of battle, losers quit and winners triumph. Be a winner! Not everybody makes it, but it is important to give it your best shot, not to despair when you don't make it, and go on to other pursuits so you can reap the benefits life has to offer.

While this book covers multiple phases of my personal life experiences, baseball became a dominant force which allowed me to meet many people and see places which otherwise would have not been possible. This book is basically a public airing of my association with the game of baseball, especially my long enduring friendship with a special group of men who played on the 1951 Schwab Pee Wee baseball team in Belleville, Ontario, Canada. Though I only coached them for that one championship season, I treasure the fond memories of the good times we had on and off the diamond. I had come into their midst as a stranger and they welcomed me with unrestrained acceptance. At the September 17, 1994 reunion of the 1951 Schwab Pee Wee baseball team members, Ted Schwab, the team sponsor, remarked to me "you know Willie, not one of those lads turned out badly." I like to think that I had a part in their development and had touched their young hearts somewhere along the way.

I had my shot at stardom and many blessings have been bestowed on me. One of my college professors said to me, "Life is filled with many pitfalls, but you will overcome them because of your great desire to succeed." Look around and realize that there are still mountains to be climbed and oceans to be crossed. Most importantly, I have accepted my station in life and have stayed the course. Rather than continuously wondering what might have been, I have accepted and recognized the realities of life as they are.

It is my pleasure and great honor to share with you the valleys and peaks in the life of a **guy who gave it his best shot**.

Table of Contents

I Gave It My Best Shot

by Willie Fordham

Overview

I Gave It My Best Shot is intended to be an inspirational work. It is designed to convince readers to do their best and not to despair if it seems they will not make it. They should go to other pursuits and reap the benefits life has to offer. Readers (especially young people) are encouraged to stay focused and never get bogged down in self-pity or regrets about what might have been. Recognizing the realities of life are the keys to success. To that end, striving to be a winner is the theme throughout the book.

SYNOPSIS

Chapter 1

THE EARLY YEARS

Described in detail are some of the author's experiences - both good and bad - while growing up in the small Pennsylvania hamlets of Millerstown and Newport. It was a time when discrimination was blatant and a cross was burned on our grandfather's front lawn. Also, it was a time when life in these rustic surroundings was crime-free, drug-free, pollution-free, and full of joy and family love.

Chapter 2

THE TEENAGE YEARS

The teenage years were spent in Carlisle, Pennsylvania, where a solid work ethic was developed as well as a world of opportunities. Pain and pleasure were experienced during these times, but there was also personal growth, both mental and social.

Chapter 3

MILITARY DUTY

Initially, induction into the Army in the fall of 1945 raised some doubts about whether or not the Army was trying to kill me. Later, the 15 months spent in Germany proved to be quite intriguing and helpful in the skills it provided for employment in the civilian world.

Chapter 4

COLLEGE DAYS

1947 - 1951 were years of immense discovery and activity that were spent at Cheyney State Teachers College in Cheyney, Pennsylvania. Upon graduation, the Athletic Director offered me the opportunity to play professional baseball in Canada, and the challenge was accepted.

Chapter 5

NORTH OF THE BORDER

Playing professional baseball in Ontario with the Oshawa Merchants and the Belleville Redmen was successful and fulfilling. Coaching a Pee Wee baseball team in Belleville led to special friendships that have lasted for the past 47 years.

Chapter 6

PRO-BALL TRYOUT

Experiences in Vero Beach, Florida during tryouts for the Brooklyn Dodgers of the Major League National Baseball team were varied and interesting, both on the field and off. Meeting veteran players like the great Jackie Robinson and hanging out with the team's Cuban players are unforgettable experiences that softened the blow of being edged out of a position on the team.

Chapter 7
CLASS AA BALL

Beginning in 1952, pitching for the professional baseball team, Harrisburg Senators, in Harrisburg, Pennsylvania provided a chance to play for a very successful Class AA team before a very supportive hometown crowd.

Chapter 8
JOB AND FAMILY LIVING

The fifties flourished with Federal employment, marriage, and children, and I became a spectator rather than a player of baseball.

Chapter 9
GREENFORD'S TV

My uncle and I start a television business. Our motto, "Our aim is to please our customers," reflected my philosophy in life to give it your best shot.

Chapter 10
KUDOS

Thanks are given to family and community for their support.

Chapter 11
NORTH OF THE BORDER AGAIN

In 1994, a Belleville, Ontario reunion with the Schwab Pee Wee baseball team members proved that time and distance did not lessen the bond we had formed 43 years ago.

Chapter 12

LIFE GOES ON

In 1994, congestive heart failure caused a brush with death that resulted in a re-evaluation of life and relationships with family members and friends.

Chapter 13

MY FAMILY MEMBERS

A capsule glance of family members is provided to show the family's solidarity and the fun times we have had together.

Chapter 14

FRIENDS

Highlights the friendships that are treasured, because of how worthwhile and fulfilling they are.

Chapter 15

FAMILY COMMENTS

The declarations of love and words of appreciation written by the immediate family.

Appendix A

REFLECTIONS

Summary of a journey filled with much joy and happiness.

Appendix B

INDEX

CHAPTER 1

The Early Years

MILLERSTOWN AND NEWPORT
Towns located in Central Pennsylvania

Mom, Dad and Me

I was born on the 15th of July 1927 in Millerstown. My parents, Daniel and Mary Fordham, separated shortly after my birth. My mother and I lived with my grandparents, John and Carrie Green; uncles, Edward and James Green; and aunts, Lucinda and Viola. Not having a father around had no adverse effect during the early years, because the Green family members filled the void through their continued love and affection for me. A love that knew no boundaries.

My grandparents' house bordered the Juniata River, where endless hours were spent swimming and floating up and down the river on an innertube. The Juniata flows to the east for 28 miles where it joins the mighty Susquehanna River at Harrisburg, Pennsylvania. At that time the Juniata was as clear as crystal and free from pollution and stagnation. My grandparent's house was a big and roomy two story white wood frame building nestled among a cluster of tall evergreen trees. It had none of today's modern conveniences such as indoor plumbing, electricity, or running water.

We had an ice box to keep our perishable foods from spoiling. A wood/coal burning stove, located in the kitchen, was used for cooking and heating water and also provided some heat in our kitchen. During the winter months, we put our personal bricks in the stove's oven to heat them for later when we would place them in our beds to warm our bodies and keep us from freezing to death. Our bedrooms, and all the other rooms in our house, were unheated. Our toilet (outhouse) was cold in the winter, so our stays there were extremely brief. The house was lighted at night by several kerosene lanterns placed strategically throughout the house. The odor of kerosene that permeated the house made us sick at times, but it was one of the trials and tribulations of life that we had to overcome; and we did survive.

A continuously flowing spring located at the rear of our house provided us with all the water we needed for cooking, drinking, and bathing. One day my brother Paul, born two years after me, was going to our spring to get water and found two large snakes swimming in the water. He dropped the two empty water buckets he was carrying and ran back to the house to tell our grandmom what happened. She picked up a garden hoe and went to the spring, killed the snakes, and filled the water buckets without as much as batting an eye. My grandmom wasn't afraid of anything, and we all knew it after being scolded, threatened, and really chastised with some good old child psychology.

The first six years of my life were spent in Millerstown. They were happy years, because the Green family was closely knit and extremely dedicated to creating a favorable environment for my uncles and me. My grandfather, John Green (we called him Pop), was an Iroquois Indian who worked on the Pennsylvania Railroad. He was a mild-mannered person whose stern glance would make me quickly mind my manners. I respected him and enjoyed spending time with him.

My grandmother, Carrie Green, ran the Green household and made sure all of us towed the line. My mom, the apparent favorite daughter, also had a firm hand in our upbringing. Mom constantly reminded me to be neat, respectful of others, and most importantly, to develop the necessary skills to become an educated individual. She also made me realize that religion should be an integral part of my upbringing. In this rustic peaceful environment, free of crime, pollution, and drugs, my life's journey began. It has been a journey that has included many memorable moments, and has resulted in my receipt of countless blessings. The significance of this is that one doesn't have to be a Jackie Robinson, Willie Mays, Babe Ruth, or Joe Louis to enjoy life to the fullest. It can be done by just being yourself. I have utilized and honed the special talents God has granted me to make my way in a world that does permit hard work and basic abilities to shine.

My Grandmother, Carrie Green

Not many blacks lived in Millerstown (two families to be exact - the Greens and the McCooks), but the early association with the white kids there appeared to be one of mutual respect. Generally, the Green family was judged by the content of its character rather than the skin color of its occupants. However, such respect was not shared by all as evidenced by an incident my mom told me about.

My Mom

My mom was an excellent student, but she told me that she stopped going to school after being advised by the principal that no black person would ever graduate from Millerstown High School. It would be quite interesting to determine if any black person did in fact graduate from Millerstown High School. I never could understand man's inhumanity against man.

At the age of six I was too busy enjoying life with my family to let people's prejudices, whether real or imagined, bother me. Bigotry in any form is unacceptable. If we examined the source of such evil we may find that the problem is that some fail to realize that we are all God made creatures with the same wants and needs.

Some in Millerstown did not approve of their black neighbors. In today's environment, the overtones of racial discontent still exist, but there are avenues of opportunity which have opened up for minorities to explore and improve their lot.

I was lucky to spend my early years in Millerstown with my uncles, Ed and Jim, who were only a few years older than I. We had many good times together and many exciting things happened. Once Ed and I buried Jim in the ground, leaving only a tube sticking out so he could breathe. We did this because Jim wouldn't play cowboys and Indians with us. He was not missed until dinner time.

Since Uncle Jim was always an early arrival at the dinner table, his absence was immediately noticed. First my grandparents, then my mom, and finally my aunts inquired about him. They looked at Ed and me, saw the sheepish grins on our faces, and quickly realized that we were the culprits responsible for Jim not being there. After we explained what happened, they all rushed out of the house to free Jim from his earthly grave. Luckily they dug him out before any serious damage was done. When freed, Jim appeared to be weak and tired, but the first words he uttered were, "I'm hungry." Ed thought Jim would retaliate against us for perpetrating this cowardly act, but Jim sort of laughed it off. It seemed, however, that every time Ed and I would be playing with our shovels, Jim would start running to one of his unknown (to us) secret hideouts. He wasn't about to let us bury him again. Even though we were tempted to repeat the act, we were fearful of the severe reprimand (including a belt strap whipping) our elders would deliver. The strong tongue lashing we received from our elders for what we had done to Jim deterred any future attempts.

There were other exciting things that happened. One day I threw a rock and accidentally broke a large plate glass window at a store front. Fortunately, no one was in the store at the time, and no one saw me throw the rock. I had always believed the police knew that I did it, so every time I saw a police car I would run home and hide under my bed because I thought they were coming to get me. That odd habit quickly disappeared when a friendly encounter with a Millerstown policeman convinced me that they did not know I had broken the window. After that, seeing a police car indicated to me that the person inside was maintaining the peace in our community, and not looking for me.

When I got into trouble I had always sought refuge in the arms of my mom and grandmom. I never told them about the rock incident because I knew they didn't have the money to pay for the broken window. To this day, I never told anyone what I had done.

Going back sixty-nine years to pull out other major events which helped shape my life is extremely difficult. Fortunately, having good buddies like my uncles, Ed and Jim, and brother Paul to pal around with seemed to have a major influence on my future development. From little acorns big oaks grow.

My grandparents' house in Millerstown is no longer standing. It was torn down many years ago to make room for a modern highway, yet the peace and tranquility in Millerstown remain with me as it was when the Greens lived there. Because I always loved the area, I later (early 1950s) purchased 35 acres of land near Seven Stars, which is approximately twenty-five miles northwest of Millerstown, from Mrs. Lottie Wilt. That was a wise investment, and even though I still own mineral rights, my plans for the land were never finalized. Owning land near my place of birth was very satisfying to me.

My grandfather, John Green, is buried at a grave site in Newport. He hated to see me bust holes in his wood frame garage at Newport with my baseball, but he never attempted to stop the battering. I guess he believed that it would be a waste of time. That garage really took a beating as a result of the pounding, yet it stood solidly for many years. When they began to use the old garage to pull engine motors from cars, that is what began its steady decline, not those lightening fast balls. I should have probably hung up an old mattress to muffle the sound and save the garage, but at the age of seven, how could one even think about such matters. The garage no longer stands, but the ringing sounds of fast balls slamming into it remain with me.

Pop, as he was called by grown-ups and children, was a kindhearted man and a highly respected faith healer. People came to our house from all over Pennsylvania to have him pray over them and "lay hands" on them. As a healer, the only town he traveled to frequently was Sunbury, PA, which is forty-five miles north of Newport. He would take all of his grandchildren along with him. We were thrilled to be riding along with our beloved Pop in one of his immense, comfortable cars. At one time, he had five of them and all were the best money could buy. We all loved and respected our grandfather very much, and he returned our love tenfold.

My grandmother, Carrie Green, was a very intelligent person who was reading William Shakespeare's works at an early age. She was an excellent student but was needed at home to help raise her eight brothers and sisters. Her mother was severely asthmatic, so Granny had to quit school in the fourth grade to milk cows, pitch hay, and help cook the family meals. She was a warm person who made friends easily, and she never said an unkind word about anyone.

The Green and McCook families often arranged big picnic parties together. There would be loads of delicious foods, and we would have a grand time talking about the good and bad happenings around town. I still remember the sweet aromas emanating from the succulent meats and homemade pastries. Everything was piled high on the picnic tables and, since the picnics lasted all day, we would beat a steady trail to the tables loaded with the mouth-watering delicacies. We laughed and played and ate until we thought our stomachs would burst open. Truly, it was the best of times.

My grandmother and Mrs. Cook would run races against each other at the picnics, and guess who won most of the time? My astonishing grandmother! She was fun to be with and was always telling us about her hard-working but fun-filled childhood. Our families would hold these picnics frequently and everyone looked forward to getting together with family and friends.

Recently revisited, I found that Millerstown has remained nearly the same over the years, with few major changes. The modern highway where my grandparents' house once stood is now a major east to west thoroughfare. Also, the once famous Millerstown Brick Factory is closed. In the suburbs many new homes have been built. To the best of my knowledge, no blacks currently live there, the place of my birth where my roots are safely buried.

Because my grandfather's railroad job relocated to Newport, the Green family moved there in 1933. Newport is located six miles east of Millerstown. We lived in a two-story wood frame house on North Front Street that was similar to our house in Millerstown. On our first night in the house, my grandparents didn't have time to set up our beds, so all of us (with the exception of my Aunt Lucinda) slept on the floor. Aunt Lucinda, whose nickname was Cindy, wasn't about to sleep on the floor, so she positioned two chairs and placed an ironing board between them. That was her bed for the first night in our new home. She was tough as nails, just like my grandmom.

Aunt Lucinda and her daughter, Wilma

Our new home was near the Pennsylvania Railroad tracks, and we knew on schedule when the trains would be barreling down the tracks. Being next to the railroad tracks, we always received copies of black newspapers, like the Pittsburgh Courier, that were thrown from the passing train conductor. The newspapers were extremely interesting and we learned a lot about the black communities of the United States. How my grandparents arranged that deal was beyond my wildest imagination, and I never bothered to ask.

At my tender young age, I could not fully comprehend what information these newspapers were providing, but I enjoyed looking at the pictures and listening to Mom talk about the famous black people mentioned in the newspapers. She said that many of the articles discussed the black man's continuous fight for equal rights, which in those days (the early 30s) were blatantly denied to black people. Unfortunately, I could not fully relate to the black man's problems because, living in Newport, I had the relative freedom to go where I pleased without any restrictions.

Just as in Millerstown, only two black families lived in Newport; the Boswells and the Greens. Being friendly with all the white kids, we weren't aware of the discrimination that may have existed in Newport. However, when it was necessary to get our hair cut, we all piled into the family car and were taken to a Harrisburg barber shop. I am not certain if my grandmother did not want to test the issue of discrimination or just used this as a means to have a grand time shopping in Harrisburg with my mother. We never challenged this practice, but it was quite strange. While in the barber shop, we saw other black people but never engaged in conversation with them. But we did not feel uncomfortable or intimidated in their presence in or out of the barber shop. In fact we really did enjoy the trips to Harrisburg and to have the opportunity to see other peoples of color – our brothers and sisters of the same ethnic background.

My Grandma and Mom shopping in Harrisburg
(while we were at the Barbershop)

Eventually, our fears, both real and imagined, concerning the issue of discrimination came into clear focus when someone set a cross on fire on my grandparents' front lawn. Granny and Pop tried to keep us from seeing such a frightening sight, but we pressed our young faces against the front window to witness the burning cross. We asked them, "Why do people hate; why do they burn crosses?" They could not offer an explanation even though they were questions that begged for an answer. What we saw was not a pretty picture. Seeing a fierce fire like the burning cross was ugly.

The following day, a stream of neighbors and local police officers came to my grandparents' house to voice their displeasure and deep concern, and they promised that those responsible would be severely punished. Unfortunately, the cowards were never apprehended, much to our dismay. If they would have decided to return, my grandfather was ready for them with his shotgun.

The Green family had never caused any problems in the community, and my grandfather was angry and astonished that someone would perpetrate this act of bigotry. The outpouring of sympathy by our neighbors and other Newport residents was comforting and we felt that those responsible for setting the cross on fire were in the minority. The incident was never repeated, however, we realized that even though there were no common outward signs of hatred and bigotry, there were members of the Newport community that harbored deep prejudices against the Green family. It may have been some dangerous neighbors up the street, but who knows.

Racial hatred in any form is intolerable and unconstitutional. While today's "laws of the land" are explicit on the matters of human rights, this incident lent credence to the fact that some ethnic groups have deep and misguided hatred toward people of color. The image of that cross burning on my grandfather's front lawn keeps coming back to me (and probably to the other members of the Green family) after all these years. That was a bad time in my life which I will never forget, but I feel sorrow for those who hate, especially those who claim to be Christians ("Christ like").

It is my opinion that persons prejudiced against people of color would certainly face their moment of truth if they witnessed one of their own:

rescued from a burning building by a fire fighter of color.
saved from drowning by a lifeguard of color.
cured of serious illness/disease by a doctor of color.
aided by a police officer of color in a dangerous or emergency situation.

I also feel sympathy for any people who have prejudices toward ethnic groups. Acceptance in the world community should be based on strength of character rather than skin color or religious beliefs or affiliations.

My grandparents had pigs and chickens that I had to feed each day. Another daily chore was picking up the eggs from the chicken coop. These tasks were irritating to my nose because of the offensive smell coming from the pens. I cleaned the eggs before giving them to my grandmom to cook. I was continuously washing my hands to get the stinky stuff off, and I also wore my high-top boots when I was in the pen, because I didn't want any of the stinky stuff getting on my good shoes. Feeding the pigs and handling the eggs were messy, bad-smelling jobs. Unfortunately, they were jobs that had to be done and I was assigned to the task. At times I did get some assistance from my uncles, Ed and Jim.

Each fall my grandfather butchered his pigs. It was a day we all enjoyed, because we knew that the meat resulting from the butchering would sustain us during the winter months. My grandparents also had fruit trees in the backyard and would can fruits picked from them. They made fresh jellies and jams for our consumption during times when the trees would no longer bear fruit. My grandmother worked very hard during the spring and summer cultivating our enormous vegetable garden that provided us with an ample supply of food all year long.

In the winter season, we all had (as in Millerstown) our personal brick which we put in the oven to

My sister, Mary, and Mom

later place in our beds to keep us warm. This was a necessity because of the lack of heating. My sister Mary (four years younger than I, who we call "Sis") had a habit of sitting in a rocking chair and rocking back and forth. One day when she was rocking near my grandmom's extremely hot stove, she fell off the chair and badly burned her hands when they came in contact with the stove. Miraculously, my grandmom healed her hands through some kind of Indian magical power. Both my grandpop and grandmom had supernatural healing powers. Many times they eased the pains I experienced just by touching the areas of pain. Their "hands on" technique really worked.

We would play strange tricks on each other. On one particular day, a trick was played on me. I was deliberately run through a pile of glass by my uncles and brother, and being barefoot at the time, I suffered injury to my right toe. My mother saw the blood squirting from the wound and almost fainted, but my grandmother calmly washed the wound with alcohol and stitched the wound with one of her sewing needles. The wound needed about ten stitches, but her operation was successful. The scar on my right toe from that incident is a constant reminder of those years spent in Newport.

My brother, Paul, was almost electrocuted by a neighbor who lived next door to my grandparents' house. Our neighbor had rigged a gadget to send electric bolts, whenever he wanted, to a fence that was used by us as a shortcut to go swimming. One day my brother was crossing the fence when it was charged with those volts, and he could not free himself from its grip. It took all of us to pull him free. To this day his hands sweat continuously as a result of that incident. In addition, this same neighbor's son hit my sister Mary with a can and it split her nose wide open. She still bears that scar today. They were dangerous, ornery, and prejudiced people.

Shortly after these crises, I decided on my own to visit my uncle John Fordham who lived in Oberlin, Pennsylvania. I hadn't seen him in a long time and wanted to visit with him and talk about my dad. I started walking towards Oberlin but eventually hitchhiked a ride to Front Street in Harrisburg (22 miles from Newport). About ten miles from my destination, and much to my dismay, I was apprehended by my mother and her future husband, Loomis Edwards. They immediately drove me back to Newport. Boy was my butt sore from that belt strap wielded by Loomis. No more runaway trips for me. I should have thought twice before setting out on my own without telling anyone and not carefully planning my trip. It was a foolish and dangerous thing to do, because anything could have happened to me. I really had the family worried about my disappearance.

Living near the Juniata River as we did in Millerstown provided the opportunity for swimming, boating, and fishing. One of our neighbors (Henry) would always come to my grandmother's house asking, "Ma, can the boys go fishing?" She always would allow us to go. Those fishing excursions with Henry, especially night carp fishing, were spectacular. We would catch a bunch and take them back to my grandmother to cook. I liked the carp eggs. We also caught eels and found them very tasty. Speaking of food, my grandmother used to feed us sugar and lard sandwiches, and we truly enjoyed them. Try one, you'll like it!

Henry would also often appear asking my grandmother, "Ma, can the boys come up to the house to play pinochle?" Again she always allowed us to go. I enjoyed the game, but I must admit that I savored the thought of eating the delicious cakes his wife, Lillian, prepared for those occasions. She was an excellent cook and pinochle player. They made us feel right at home and we looked forward to spending time with them. Henry would always return us to our house within the allotted time given to him by our grandmother.

Christmas around the homestead, as we lovingly called it, was exciting. One Christmas day I broke off my front tooth on the door handle while attempting to peer through the keyhole in the dark. Boy did my mom scold me. After that, we had to wait until permission was granted to us to unwrap our presents. The presents and scrumptious dinner that followed are frequently the subject of conversation between my siblings and me. The delicious smells of food cooking included corn bread, stuffing, mashed potatoes, and many baked goods. It permeated throughout the house and whetted our appetites.

We had a German shepherd named Rover that I used to hitch up to our sled for a fun-filled snowy ride. It was amazing to see how he could pull all of us packed precariously on the sled. Rover was a good dog and was very protective of us. Each day after school I had fun playing with Rover while also feeding the pigs and chickens.

In Newport at the age of seven, my love for the game of baseball began. Throwing a baseball seemed to be a natural thing for me to do. I always made time in the evenings to throw the baseball through a tire I had hung on my grandfather's garage. It was a daily routine that I would do for an hour, and soon the baseball was being thrown at great velocity through the tire. Mom kept telling me, "Boy, you are going to throw your arm off." Amazingly, my arm was sound and gave me no trouble. Even though

My Grandfather

the garage took a beating, and Pop cringed each time I busted holes in it, the garage and tire provided the experience I needed to perform successfully at the professional level later in life.

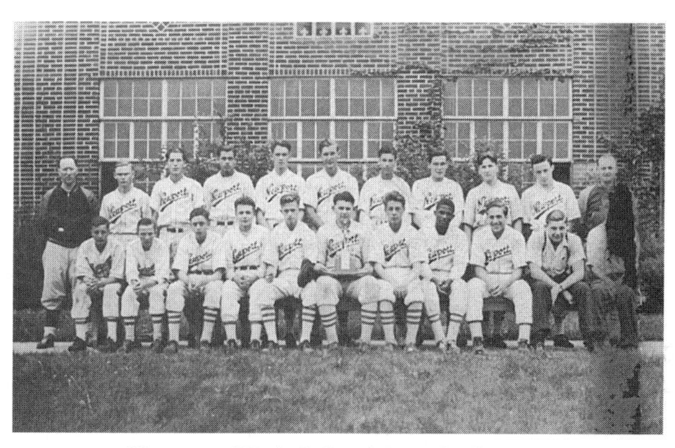

Newport High School Baseball Team
(I am the only Black team member)

My pitching record for the Newport High School team was good. Once out there on the mound I would pretend that I was pitching baseballs through that old tire hung on my grandfather's garage. Billy Cox, a former baseball star for the Harrisburg Senators of the Eastern League and later the Brooklyn Dodgers of the major National Baseball League, also played for the Newport High baseball team at shortstop.

The flood of 1936 left the homestead, which was held together by wood pegs, in a state of shambles. Water and mud were everywhere, and we had to move to higher ground until the water subsided. Thanks to our neighbors, we were provided temporary housing. I can clearly remember that big pot of chicken corn soup and other necessities they provided for us. We generally had good neighbors who looked out for one another, and they all ignored the dangerous neighbors up the street who were obnoxious toward their black neighbors. Luckily, their narrow-minded views were not popular among other citizens of Newport.

On weekends, all of us going to the local movie house

was a favorite treat. That big lion appearing on the screen was scary, and it took all of them to calm me. One particular weekend, we complained to our grandmother that we did not want to see the movie that was scheduled to be shown because we had seen that same movie previously. She went to the movie manager requesting that a different movie be shown, one that would please her family. The manager complied and we all enjoyed the substitute move that featured cowboy Tom Mix. To this day, I do not know how my grandmother pulled that stunt. My grandmother was a wonderful person and well-liked in the community. On another trip to the movies, a car ran over my foot and I sat on the curb rocking my body back and forth holding my foot and moaning. When the pain subsided, I proceeded to go to the movies with my family members.

Granny was a very religious person. Come rain or shine, each Sunday we went to the Evangelical Church on Fourth Street to attend religious services.

One summer a train carrying circus animals derailed and overturned near Newport. Word got out that an alligator had escaped from the wreckage and was seen in the Juniata River near our swimming area. Well, I decided that that was the end of my swimming for the summer, but not my Aunt Lucinda. She wasn't scared of an alligator and continued to swim daily in the Juniata without incident. I joined my tough-as-nails aunt in her daily swimming, but you can bet my eyes were wide open as I searched for that missing gator. Can you imagine what it would be like being face-to-face with an alligator on its own turf? I did not want to find out. The alligator scare lasted for the remainder of the summer; however, the alligator never appeared.

I purchased the old homestead from my grandmother in the 1950s to keep my boyhood experiences alive. Each year our families returned to the homestead for one day of picnicking, drinking, fighting, and reminiscing about the good old days. The homestead is no longer there, and the land was sold to others. Nevertheless, fond memories of my early teen-age days spent there with my relatives are permanently etched in my memory bank.

In 1944 I moved to Carlisle to live with my mother, stepfather, brother, and sister. My stepfather, Loomis, found employment in Carlisle and asked us to join him there. Leaving Newport was sad because of my roots there and in Millerstown. On the way to Carlisle I wondered what challenges I would be facing and how I would react. It didn't take long to find out. The change in environment would certainly require some major adjustments in this country boy's life-style.

CHAPTER 2

The Teenage Years

CARLISLE
Town located in Central Pennsylvania

Arriving in Carlisle, which is about thirty miles south of Newport, I got a rude awakening. It was a real wake-up call. Some members of my ethnic group were using the 4-letter F--- word, and others were being loud and rowdy. Since I was accustomed to the peace and quiet of country living and unaccustomed to this type of behavior, a state of shock set in. Even attending the local black church was a different experience for me. For instance, on one occasion some members of the church became highly emotional, and I ran out of the church. In Newport, the only voice you heard was that of the preacher giving the sermon. It became obvious that a major adjustment in my life-style had to be made mentally, socially, and quickly.

The mental adjustment was less complex. My sense of values honed into me by my family during the earlier years in Millerstown and Newport never changed. Because of my shy personality, I neither resorted to using cuss words nor became rowdy or disrespectful to others. Socially, many changes had to be made. Being among members of my own race made their acceptance of me extremely important. I attended their dances but was a wall flower because I did not know how to dance (and still have not learned).

I had never dated a black female, and my shyness made even talking to them extremely difficult. All of my previous female friends were white, and with them I felt very comfortable. As a result, I have no problem with interracial dating. To each his own. But, eventually I had many memorable moments with my black female friends, and in time, felt just as comfortable with them as with my white female friends in Millerstown and Newport.

My first order of priority was getting a job to finance the purchase of an automobile. Several job opportunities opened up, resulting in steady employment. My first job was washing cars in a local garage; second was driving a dump truck; third was working as a bell hop at the Molly Pitcher hotel; and fourth was shining shoes. These were learning experiences and were the basis for a good work ethic which I have continued throughout my life. It has been very important that I developed good work habits at an early age to reap the benefits society has to offer.

Before my 17th birthday I owned my first car. It was a 1935 Ford, and I had paid cash ($250.00) for it. When my mom saw the car, she became concerned and feared I would have an accident with it. My driving instructor, Mrs. Williams, taught me how to drive it in one week. I passed my driving test on the first attempt and realized that receiving my driver's license afforded me a new sense of independence.

Frequently, I would drive to Newport to visit the family members who had remained there. On one of these trips, I returned to Carlisle with my Aunt Lucinda's son, Genaro, who was two years old with hair down to his shoulders. Without her permission, I took him to a local barber shop. While I have no problem with long hair, Genaro looked too much like a little girl to suit me. Because he would not sit still in the barber chair, the barber and others had to calm him. I thought he looked more boyish and much better after the haircut. Unfortunately, all h--- broke out when his mom saw him. She ran after me hollering "Wilbur, I am going to get you for this!" Fortunately, she never caught up to me. I honestly believe she never forgave me for that act.

My Aunt Lucinda prepared meals for the Washington Redskins professional football team for many years during their pre-season training camp stay in Carlisle. She specialized in Mexican cuisine. She is gone now, but I treasure the fond memories of the good days spent with her in Millerstown, Newport, and Carlisle. Her daughters, Wanda and Wilma, still reside in Carlisle, but Genaro, who graduated from Temple University Medical School, died while practicing medicine in Philadelphia and is greatly missed by the family.

Carlisle presented a world of opportunities for me such as my ownership of the Ford car, steady employment, and apparent acceptance by my ethnic friends. These friends helped me tremendously to adapt to the new surroundings. One friend had a television set in his home. Each Friday night, when the boxing matches would come on, he would invite me to watch them. His family was one of a few in Carlisle that had a television set at that time. Later on, I was the best man at his wedding. He is a prince, a super star, but most importantly a true friend; his name is James (Bud) Oakley. We spent many good times together traveling to various nearby towns (Gettysburg, Lewistown, Mt. Union) in the good old Ford. He also helped me get out of a couple of incidents with some town bullies who liked to throw their weight around. Fortunately, having been on the boxing team in Newport, these physical incidents could be handled. At Newport High School I was the boxing champion in my weight class;

however, having Bud around as my backup was comforting.

God above sent me a beautiful sister.

I was very protective of my sister, Mary, whom we call Sis. She is a very attractive person, and I can recall the day when she came home wearing some guy's sweater. I demanded to know just what she thought she was doing and took that sweater over to the fellow's house and told him never again to give my sister anything. In her innocence, she did not understand my action, but from the day she was born I always felt that it was my responsibility to protect her. I had trouble realizing that Sis had a mind of her own and was capable of making her own decisions. She, like I, had a strong sense of values honed into her by her elders. Her husband (Bunce) and one of her daughters (Monica) have passed this life. She has a daughter named Jessica, and several grandchildren, two of which she raised from birth. Her grandson, Jaman, graduated with honors from Slippery Rock University. Sis, my wife, and I attended his graduation ceremony.

My brother, Paul, adapted to the Carlisle environment much more quickly than I because of his outgoing nature. He had many friends. He was a good worker and also had steady employment. I can remember the day I took him and our cousin, William Latham (Bunchie), in the old Ford to Newport to visit the homestead. Playing those tricks we used to pull in Newport, they stole my car. Neither had a driver's license. When I finally caught up with them, they were laughing and having a good time. The incident was quickly forgotten, and they never resorted to such underhanded tactics again. Afterwards, much to their chagrin, I told them that I didn't condone their actions and punished them by not allowing them to sit or ride in my car for three months.

Paul was a good jockey and had horses, Major, and Glamor Girl. Mom was very concerned that he would have an accident, and he actually did have a serious spill with Major that terrified her. Paul and his wife, Kathryn, are proud parents of Christopher, Lance, and Crystal, and have several grandchildren.

During my senior year at Carlisle High School, I pitched a no-hit baseball game and had a season record of 8 wins and no losses. I was the only black on the team. The no-hit baseball game was one of the highlights of my life. After the last pitch and the last batter was struck out, a sense of quiet reflection settled over me. My teammates kept pounding me on the back and hugging me to show their appreciation for the tremendous effort I had put forth. After the no-hit game, my teammates took me to a local restaurant to celebrate our victory. There I tasted an incident of discrimination. Shortly after we arrived, all of my white teammates were given menus to select the items of their choice. I did not receive a menu and it became immediately apparent that the restaurant would not serve me. Obviously, it was because I was black. After seeing that I was being ignored I decided to leave the restaurant. All of the team members followed me with tears in their eyes. They all tried, in a sympathetic way, to console and assure me that they were embarrassed by this incident.

The hurt and embarrassment resulting from the incident left a bitter taste in my mouth. I had just pitched our high school baseball team to a no-hit victory, which is considered a significant feat. However, I could not enjoy the victory by dining with my teammates. I could understand if I was not served because of some erratic behavior I had exhibited, but being rejected solely on the basis of my black skin just did not make sense. My teammates suggested that we file a formal protest, but in those years that would have been an exercise in futility. The apparent theme during that time was "separate but equal." The restaurant incident was disgusting, but it did not dampen my enthusiasm to succeed.

My mother was very proud of my accomplishments, but was also hurt when she learned of what had happened at the restaurant. After discussing it with her, she explained that all white people were not prejudiced. That fact became quite evident, because I have personally been involved with many white people whom I believe have accepted me based on the content of my character. The 1951 Schwab Pee Wee baseball team members, which I talk about in detail in Chapter 5, were all white and are a classic example of that fact.

Many people lie daily in the sun to acquire my skin color. Thank God my color is built in permanently. Black people must fully realize that we are a beautiful God-made creation. My mom and grandmom always taught me to "do unto others as you would have them do unto you." This has been my modus operandi over the years. I am proud to be a black man because my ancestors had to be strong and brave to withstand the brutal punishment (both to mind and body) delivered by the slave masters. Also, I am keenly aware that some of my ancestors were of royal heritage in their native African homeland. There is a strong sense of pride knowing that the blood flowing within me is rich in historical significance, just as Rev. Jesse Jackson, a civil rights leader, encourages us to believe that "we are somebody."

Once again, out there on the mound pitching for the Carlisle High School baseball team, I could always pretend that the baseballs were being thrown through that old car tire hung on my grandfather's garage. As expected, that experience did prove valuable. The speed on my fast ball increased tremendously, and I was extremely accurate in getting the baseball over the plate. The local newspapers in Carlisle published many stories about my success on the diamond.

Usually, when one stands out in any given sport, recognition comes easily and eager scouts attempt to sign you up, but none came my way. "Why not?" remains a question. Maybe we all should have been born color blind.

Prior to my graduation from Carlisle High School, my mother bought me a new brown suit which I wore proudly. She was a good mom. I can remember a day that I was returning to Cheyney State College and I had forgotten my winter jacket at home. As I was about to turn the corner, there came Mom huffing and puffing with my jacket. She knew it would be needed during the winter months at Cheyney and had run (at full speed) a half a block to make sure I got it before I departed. I know that many moms would do that, but I believe mine was one of the best anywhere in the world.

When I introduced my wife, Jessie, to her for the first time, Mom accepted her graciously and without reservation. She even gave me the diamond ring that my father, Daniel, had given to her, to give to Jessie. My wife still has that ring even though it is no longer wearable. She plans to have the diamond reset in another ring.

Mom was a good cook and served big tasty mouth-watering meals, especially during the holiday seasons. She is gone now, but I never have forgotten how she taught me to cope with the ups and downs in life. She instilled in me a sense of pride and gave me a vivid image of what is right and what is wrong. Most importantly she set a good example for me to follow.

My grandmother, Carrie Green, lived to be 97 years of age. She lived in my mother's house in Carlisle for many years prior to her death. Each November when my sons were growing up, she would accompany my mother and me to Philadelphia to purchase Christmas presents for them. I got a 15% discount at one particular store, because I personally knew the owner's son. Prior to our return, and after loading the gifts into my vehicle, Mom and my grandmother did a little shopping and sight-seeing on their own. We always dined at one of the better restaurants there; then, we would go home to Carlisle where they spent endless hours wrapping all those gifts and making sure that name tags were attached properly on each one. Watching them doing this convinced me that their efforts were a labor-of-love, and that they knew the wrappings were a part of the gift.

On Christmas Eve I would drive from Harrisburg to Carlisle, pick up the gifts, and safely sneak them into our house on Calder Street while my young chargers were sound asleep. Come Christmas morning, all h--- broke out. The wrapping came off their gifts faster than Mom and Granny put them on, as they eagerly went to work seeing what Santa had brought them. I wondered why they would wrap those gifts in the first place. Their labor-of-love efforts quickly evaporated with the first tugs at the wrappings. Their time spent wrapping and marking the gifts is a constant reminder that I had two very special people in my life, my mom and grandmother. They seemed to make life worthwhile and fulfilling. They still are my champions – my heroes.

In June of 1945, I graduated from Carlisle High School, and guess who I got a letter from in December 1945? The President of the United States (Harry Truman) requested me to report for military service. I was frustrated and couldn't help but think that I was only a young man of 18, having the time of my life and enjoying the company of my family, when something like this had to happen. Regretfully, when the President wants you, you get your bags packed. Also, I was puzzled by the fact that I could not sit in a local restaurant, but I was good enough to sit in a military vehicle.

Leaving my family was sad because of close associations. Even though I was going, my roots remained safely buried in Millerstown and Newport. What could I expect during my tour of duty with the United States Army? This question was quickly answered upon arrival at Camp Kilmer in New Jersey.

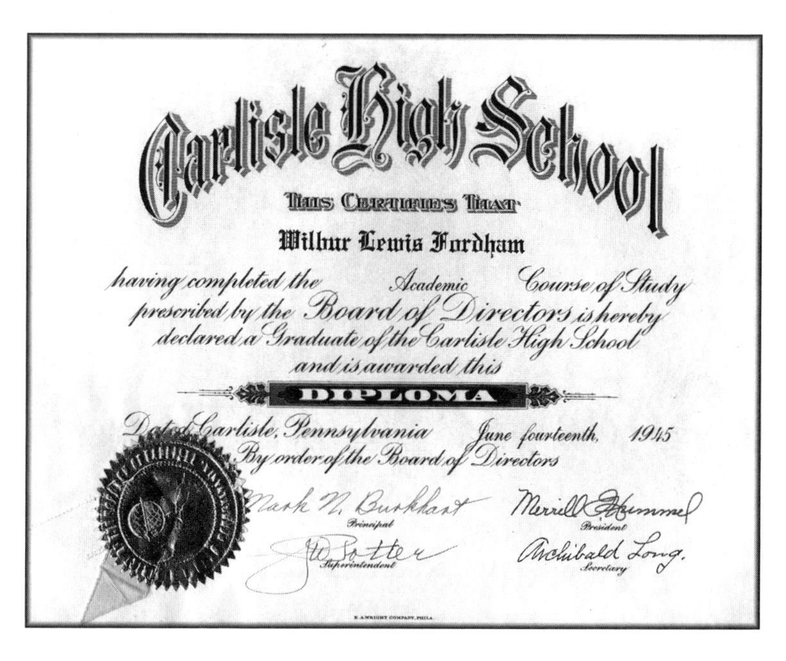

Carlisle High School

This Certifies That

Wilbur Lewis Fordham

having completed the Academic Course of Study prescribed by the Board of Directors is hereby declared a Graduate of the Carlisle High School and is awarded this

DIPLOMA

Dated Carlisle, Pennsylvania June fourteenth, 1945

By order of the Board of Directors

Mark N. Burkhart
Principal

Merrill K. Hummel
President

J W Potter
Superintendent

Archibald Long.
Secretary

My Carlisle High School Diploma

New Arrivals, Camp Kilmer, N.J.

Post Headquarters, Camp Kilmer, N.J.

CHAPTER 3

Military Duty

THE UNITED STATES ARMY
Camp Kilmer, New Jersey
Fort Lewis, Washington
Verdun Concern, Geissen, Germany

In early December 1945, I bade farewell to my family and was drafted into the United States Army at Camp Kilmer. When the officer asked me which service I preferred, I replied the Navy; however, I was assigned to the Army (my uncle Jim had served in the U.S. Navy for many years, and my brother Paul served in the U.S. Army for two years in Northern Japan as a Telecommunications Specialist 3rd Class). I have always wondered what would have happened if I had said I wanted to serve in the Army. The officer's question was academic, because he knew my service assignment before he asked the question. It didn't take long for me to realize that the military had set plans for its inductees.

At the time of my induction, the U.S. Armed Forces were segregated. As a result, I was in an all black squad that was assigned to Fort Lewis in Washington State. There we received our basic training. Not only did we experience brief rain showers off and on daily, but we also had several small earthquakes that came rumbling through our barracks on occasion. We took all unforeseen incidents in stride and considered them to be minor and just another example of what we should expect during our tour of duty in the Army.

Our barracks were big and roomy. We were continually cleaning up our sleeping area in preparation for our weekly inspection by the Commanding General. We kept our shoes shined and our beds neatly made up. Consistently, our barracks always passed those inspections.

The cleaning of our M1 rifles was a difficult and extremely dangerous task for many of the troops, especially if your thumb got caught in the trigger mechanism. Some received severe thumb injuries that required a visit to the base hospital. Fortunately, I was able to handle and load the M1 rifle. It was a heavy piece of equipment that was later replaced by the M16 Carbine, a much lighter weapon. I became skilled in the handling of a rifle and eventually became a squad leader.

We began each day with a three mile jog in full battle gear. It was an exhausting task. I silently wondered if the Army was trying to kill us, even before we could use our fighting machine skills in some foreign land.

We were given detailed training in the art of modern warfare. We would go on long hikes and use a compass to find our way through forest areas leading back to the base camp. We continually practiced our parade drill formations. Looking at that grand old Mt. Rainier from the parade grounds impressed all the troops. After the end of our daily exercises we were dismissed. The officers would holler, "Carry on!" which in Army parlance means "Go about your business as usual!"

At first, being away from home was disturbing, but

as time went by we adjusted to our new environment and were learning to become skilled warriors in Uncle Sam's Army – an Army which had no equal.

After six weeks, we were declared physically and mentally fit to carry out our assigned military duties. After basic training was completed, we boarded the General Walker troop carrier for our overseas destination in Geissen, Germany. We were advised by the medical personnel aboard to eat chocolate candy bars to prevent seasickness. I heeded this advice and it worked. There was no sickness for me on the way to Germany or on the return trip home. Some guys didn't believe in this remedy and got sick.

In the U.S. Army Uniform

Viewing the Atlantic ocean from the ship, and not seeing land in either direction, was both breathtaking and scary. I was proud to be a member of the Armed Forces sent to Germany to maintain the peace, but at the same time, I was sad to be leaving family and friends. We passed the White Cliffs of Dover on the way and were in awe of their majestic beauty. The cliffs appeared to be touching the blue sky above. Soon after passing the cliffs, we landed at Bremerhaven, Germany and were taken to the Verdun Concern, which would be my home for the next 15 months.

My assignment was in the master control switchboard room handling incoming and outgoing telephone calls. It proved to be a very interesting job. Since my duties were performed at night, the fellows in the kitchen would send over tasty meals to tide me over until breakfast.

In the daytime, I was in charge of the Concern's gasoline depot. It actually was not bad, because my office was well-heated at all times. Most of my duties were performed outdoors, and the danger of a gas explosion was always present. All gasoline issued/consumed was recorded on detailed entry logs in my office. When we needed fuel, I pulled as many trucks as needed from the trucking pool and loaded them with empty five gallon cans for the trip to the major fuel resupply depot located in Frankfort, Germany for refill. All loading/off-loading operations of the five gallon gas cans was done by German prisoners, and I never had any problems with them.

Life in Germany for our squad members had its ups and downs. We visited the few remaining local business establishments. Unfortunately, as in Carlisle, discrimination raised it's ugly head. Some German girls were still checking our butts to see if we actually did have tails. It seems that false assumption was planted in the German's minds years ago. It was not hard to determine how that false story was promulgated. The German men were just curious, which is natural because of the cultural and ethnic differences existing between us.

Everywhere we went we saw a familiar sign, "Kilroy was here!" It seemed old Kilroy was always one stop ahead of everybody. All throughout my military career that Kilroy sign was in every nook and cranny. I sure would like to have met him one day. However, that probably would have been an impossible task, because he would always be gone before I got there.

The food served in the kitchens was edible, especially on Thanksgiving and Christmas, but oh that German coffee! It was bitter and strong, but at least it warmed you. Their black bread was different, the beer was excellent, and overall we got enough to eat. The packages from home were always tasty because of the TLC (tender loving care) that was thrown in. Mail arrived in bunches and contained details of the happening back home. The mail I sent home usually was comprised of a gift, such as money or jewelry, to let my folks know that I had not forgotten about them.

I gave a German artist a black and white picture card of my mother and asked to have it converted into something colorful. To my surprise, he painted her picture in color in a large wooden frame. It was truly a work of art, and Mom was delighted when she received it. It still hangs in her home in Carlisle and was one of her prized possessions.

Winters in Germany were brutal and long-lasting. The barracks we lived in were solidly constructed and insulated. As a result, we stayed warm and comfortable in them.

It was sad to see how Germany fared in the war. Many burned out buildings still stood, and the landscape was devastated. However, remembering that Germany began the war, it received the severe punishment it deserved. Yet, it is amazing that Germany survived in the wake of the tremendous battering it received from the allied forces. Germany today is at relative peace with the world.

The German citizens were dressed poorly and were constantly begging for food. I gave much of my candy rations to them, especially the children, who would eagerly gobble down the treats and ask for more. Getting treats, plus sharing some of the food items I would get from home, kept my little German friends happy. Since I didn't smoke, my cigarette rations were traded for candy items that could also be given to the German children. The German ladies were friendly with the Black troops, but I personally never got too friendly with them. The fear of diseases they may be carrying often entered my mind, thus I abstained from contact with them. German men looked at us with scorn but realized that there was nothing they could do to end their misery; the U.S. occupation troops were there to stay and had complete control over them.

The tour of Germany lasted approximately 15 months. I was assigned to the 3410 Truck Corp. Its function was carrying supplies and troops where needed. I can remember the day our squad was assigned to deliver some jeeps to a far away destination in the dead of winter. Those jeeps had no heaters and it was bitter cold. We arrived at our destination and delivered the jeeps, but we suddenly realized that no provisions had been made for our return trip to our home base. After several frantic days, our outfit caught up to us with transportation for the trip back to the base. Army blunders do occur.

Nightly guard duty for all the troops was required to patrol the perimeter of the Concern and be on alert for snipers and intruders. Fortunately, no serious incidents occurred. My relations with my fellow Black comrades were good. We seemed to have a good rapport; possibly because we were all together in a strange foreign land and homesick. Whenever we learned that someone lived in the same town or nearby in the States, we would call each other "Homeboy".

With friends in Germany

Near the end of my stay in Germany, my Commander asked if I would like to sign up for a six year tour of duty. My reply was "Don't call me. I'll call you!" I wanted to get out of that man's Army ASAP. I did, however, meet many people with whom I shared some fun times and saw places in Germany which would not have been possible as a civilian. Also, the rigors of Army life and the discipline required proved valuable to me later in life. Serving in Uncle Sam's Army provided funds through the G. I. Bill for my college education. I would urge young people to get their high school diploma and join one of the U.S. Armed Forces. The military service will provide the basic skills and fundamentals of various high-tech trades that will be needed to attend schools of higher education and possible later entrance into the civilian work force.

Young people must be involved in the educational environment and advised to abstain from the use of drugs, alcohol, and other addictive substances. Young people are vulnerable to all kinds of vices. They may not understand that it is unwise to respond to peer pressure. The reliance on their own set of values will steer them to their select peer group. There must be a development of inner strength where your own set of values are your peer group.

I was glad to leave Germany knowing that soon I would be returning to my family and friends in the good old USA. I silently wondered how things had changed in Carlisle during my absence and what major adjustments would be needed on my part to resume my pre-Army life-style, a life-style that had brought me much enjoyment and memory.

When I am financially able, I would like to revisit Germany to see again the places where I was stationed during my service with the U.S. Army.

CHAPTER 4

College Days

CHEYNEY STATE TEACHERS COLLEGE
Cheyney, Pennsylvania

Shortly after my discharge from the U.S. Army, I sat around Carlisle pondering what my future would hold. That was when Dean James Fraiser, a Cheyney professor who lived in Carlisle, contacted my friend, Edgar Gumby, and me about attending that college. I discussed it with my family, and it was decided that I had everything to gain and nothing to lose by going to Cheyney.

Located approximately eighty miles east of Harrisburg, the college is one of the oldest historically Black institutions of higher learning in the United States.

Packing up the 1941 Desoto that I had purchased after my military service ended, Ed and I drove to Cheyney to begin our college studies. We were both highly motivated by the fact that Cheyney was virgin territory for us, and we were uncertain about what campus life had in store for us.

Students were not allowed to have cars on campus

during their freshman year; as a result, the Desoto was returned to Carlisle. On the way back, it developed serious motor problems and had to be put into a local garage for repairs.

To my dismay, I quickly learned that Cheyney did not field a baseball team, but that problem was quickly resolved. I hooked up with a professional baseball team (Meteors) in Philadelphia, where I earned extra money on the weekends. Playing with the Meteors was my first opportunity to play professional baseball. It was exciting to play with skilled ball players, many who had the skills to play in the major leagues. I can't remember the names of the fellows I played with, but they treated me as one of their own. Many indicated that I was a promising candidate for a successful baseball career. Once again, out there on the mound in Philadelphia, I pretended that the horsehide was being thrown through the old tire that hung on my grandfather's garage.

Campus life at Cheyney during my Freshman year was hectic. We were continually harassed, made fun of, and forced to do stupid things. The only consolation I had was knowing that this would end, and that someday I would be able to reciprocate.

Dr. Leslie Pickney Hill (in his office)

Ed and I joined the Cheyney Choir lead by the late Dr. Leslie Pickney Hill. Dr. Hill was also the President and founder of the college. I enjoyed singing with the other members who had magnificent voices. We sang at many concerts during my stay with the choir, which lasted for the four years I spent at Cheyney. Dr. Hill's poem, "The Teacher", follows:

THE TEACHER

Lord, who am I to teach the way,
To little Children day by day,
So prone myself to go astray.

I teach them Knowledge, but I know,
How faint they flicker, and how low,
The candles of my knowledge glow.

I teach them Power to will and do,
But only now to learn anew,
My own great weakness through and through.

I teach them Love for all mankind,
And all God's creatures, but I find,
My love comes lagging far behind.

Lord, if their guide, I still must be,
Oh, let the little children see,
The teacher leaning hard on thee.

–Leslie Pickney Hill

In addition to singing in the choir, I played on the Cheyney basketball team that had many good players. My academic studies were interesting and presented a challenge to my intelligence. These studies were a step above those learned in high school.

The first year at Cheyney went by swiftly. One snowy winter night around 8:00 p.m., I got homesick. Not having a car, I asked a student friend, Sidney DeKnight to take me home for a visit. He grumbled a bit, but minutes later we were in his Ford heading toward Carlisle. I never will forget his act of kindness. Sidney passed away early in 1994, but the memory of his true friendship over the years is everlasting. My only regret is I did not get a chance to tell him goodbye. His wife Jackie and daughter Sylvia still reside in Philadelphia and we stay in contact. My children called him "Uncle Sid," and my family loved him. He visited us many times and even attended the wedding of my son, Steve. Very neat in appearance and always the gentleman, Sidney also was an accomplished musician. He was a retired teacher and music director in many churches in and around Philadelphia all his life. Rest in peace dear friend.

My 1941 Desoto

My second year at Cheyney was without incident, and this time I got the chance to harass the Freshman class members. Also, that same year as I was walking one day from my Tanglewood room to the campus, I heard a horn blowing. Lo and behold there was my brother, Paul, with my old Desoto and a big smile on his face. Knowing that I loved that car, he paid the garage bill with his personal funds and brought the car to me. He never asked for one cent of the repair bill, which I found out later was over $300.00. Quite a sum of money in the 50s. How many brothers would pay a brother's car bill and not ask for a cent in return? In addition, my brother had loaned me his car to return to Cheyney while my Desoto was in the garage for repair. I will never forget his act of kindness.

That Desoto provided a steady source of funds. My taxi services for the professors and students, to and from the local train station, were profitable and kept me supplied with the necessities. As a bonus, it became a good source for liaisons with the female students on campus and as transportation to my part-time job, which was five miles away.

I met several other friends, both female and male, whose friendships I have treasured. Mrs. Lois Maloney, a close family friend, also graduated from Cheyney and she keeps in touch. My wife is her son Greg's godmother.

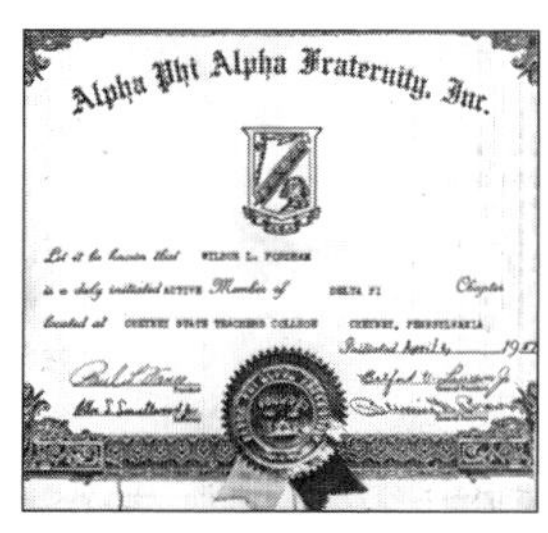
Alpha Phi Alpha Fraternity, Inc.

My Alpha Phi Alpha Fraternity Certificate

In my junior year the Alpha Phi Alpha (AϕA) fraternity accepted me as a member. This organization has provided the avenues for my participation in many social and fraternal activities. There is a chapter in Harrisburg. In our dear AϕA, fraternal spirits bind all the noble, the true and courageous.

On line with my Alpha Phi Alpha (AϕA) *Fraternity Brothers*

I also began my first session of student teaching at the Coopin School located near Cheyney's campus during my junior year. It was interesting to learn that the techniques learned in classroom studies really worked at Coopin. The young students were eager to learn, and you could see their eyes light up as you carried them through one story after another. They treated me with respect and really wanted to learn the various subjects we studied.

My graduation picture (1951)

In my senior year it was more of the same, classroom studies and more student teaching. On May 30, 1951, I received my Bachelor of Science Degree from Cheyney State Teachers College.

Before I left campus after graduation, I was approached by our Athletic Director, William O'Shields, asking if I wanted to go to Canada to play professional baseball. He explained that there was a professional team in Oshawa, Ontario, Canada looking for Black American ball players. Without hesitation, I accepted the offer. Coach O'Shields also gave me $25.00 for traveling expenses. He was not only my coach, but a friend.

The four years spent at Cheyney made me realize the important role of teachers. They teach the way to little children day by day. I left Cheyney with a sense of pride with my Bachelor of Science degree, looking forward to meeting the challenges which lie ahead.

Going to Canada to play professional baseball would be my first challenge after graduation. I wondered what reception the Canadians had planned for me.

Cheyney Graduation Ceremony

COMMONWEALTH OF PENNSYLVANIA

133021

DEPARTMENT OF PUBLIC INSTRUCTION

COLLEGE CERTIFICATE

Know all men by these presents *that* WILBUR LEWIS FORDHAM *a graduate of* Cheyney Training School *with the degree of* B. S. in Education *having filed with the Department of Public Instruction satisfactory evidence of the requisite qualifications, is hereby granted this Certificate and is authorized to teach for three years in the public schools of this Commonwealth the subjects prescribed for the curriculum of the elementary school* having specialized in the Intermediate Field

In Testimony Whereof *the Superintendent of Public Instruction has hereunto set the seal of the Department of Public Instruction and affixed his signature at Harrisburg, this* 11th *day of* June *AD 1951*

Made Permanent ______ 19__

Superintendent of Public Instruction

Superintendent of Public Instruction

Commonwealth of Pennsylvania College Certificate

CHAPTER 5

North of the Border

THE CANADA EXPERIENCE
Oshawa, Ontario, Canada
Belleville, Ontario, Canada

In the first week of June 1951, I arrived in Oshawa with great anticipation. I met with the team owner and began to work out with my teammates. The team was comprised mostly of Canadians with a sprinkle of Americans. I was the only Black, and there were a few Puerto Ricans. It was called the Oshawa Merchants, and the Americans on the team were called imports. The team traveled throughout Ontario playing professional baseball teams at the Class AA level.

My stay in Oshawa was short. Officials from the Belleville Redmen professional team offered me a position with their team. I pitched many games for the Redmen, which was a rather good baseball team. Johnny Dean (a catcher) and I were the only Blacks on the team. After one particular game that I had had a big hand in winning, a newspaper article was written by the sports editor, George Carver, that depicted me as a guy who could "tread water without getting wet." I was very appreciative of the complimentary article he wrote. Later, I received a key to the city.

Going to Belleville was a blessing in disguise, because it was at Belleville that I came in contact with a special group of white lads, ages 11 through 13, called the Schwab Pee Wee baseball team. One day after practice, Ted Schwab, owner of a novelty shop and sponsor of the Schwab Pee Wee baseball team, asked me to coach this team. After I accepted the challenge, I began to wonder about the kind of kids I would be coaching. What would their personalities be like? What about their impression of me? After all, I was a stranger in their midst, so would I be accepted?

All the bad things I anticipated did not exist. From our first meeting until my departure from Canada, these young lads and I developed a special friendship that has lasted over the past forty-three years. What made this player/coach relationship click? First of all, they were eager to learn the game of baseball. Having seen me perform for the Redmen, they may have felt that I was the right guy to lead them to victories. Anyway, it was time to whip them into shape and get them ready to play ball.

Immediately, I found that they needed more equipment to perform, so I visited Mr. Schwab and told him of our equipment needs (balls, bats, shoes, gloves, etc.). His reply to me was "Willie, take what you need." When you have a team sponsor like Ted, you are obligated to do everything possible to make his team a winning one. And win it did! I cannot remember one game they lost under my guidance. This is not intended to boast, but only underscore the tremendous athletic abilities of my young friends. They did everything I asked them to do and more.

There were many mornings around 6:00 a.m. when all the Schwab Pee Wee team members came to Mrs. Hall's house on 10 Earle Street where I lived hollering, "Get up

Willie. Let's go play ball." It was difficult to arise from my deep sleep but how could I let down those bright and eager lads. So, I got up and went with them to the practice field and practice we did from sun up to sun down. However, it paid off. On the field they perfected their baseball skills to such an extent that Ted Schwab and their parents were amazed, and so was I. The parents' support of the team was fantastic. They attended all the games and were very vocal in rooting the team on to victory.

Time Capsule
Ted Schwab contributed this 1951 photograph of Schwab's Pee Wee baseball club. Schwab's Stationery sponsored the team, which played in a league with other squads such as Walker's Hardware and Lattimer's Drugs. Front row from left, catcher D. Coe, left fielder J. Meagher, pitcher J. Elliott; second row, first base R. Hurst, second R. Alexander, centre fielder R. Keller, infielder A. Barclay; back row, coach W. Fordham, right field J. Warren, coach T. Cathcart, short stop S. Schwab, outfielder J. Foster, third base N. Rushlowe, sponsor Ted Schwab.

Schwab Pee Wee Baseball Team (1951)

Our pitcher had a fancy curve ball that he liked to throw frequently. I told him to knock off throwing all those curve balls, because he would ruin his young arm. I told him to resort to a change-of-speed pitch, but old habits are hard to break. He was an excellent pitcher and kept us close in all games. I only had to tell them once what to do; no repeat instruction was necessary. They took to the diamond like a duck to water.

My association with my young chargers did not end on the diamond. They invited me to their homes to meet their families and have dinner. It seems that every waking hour was spent with them when I was not pitching for the Redmen.

We took long hikes out in the country, read inspirational books and generally did things to sharpen our mental as well as our physical facilities. I really enjoyed the good times we spent together on and off the diamond, and the question and answer periods we held in the dugout. Prior to our daily practices, we would be in the dugout covering a wide range of subjects to enhance their memory banks. They enjoyed these sessions.

Never in my life had I allowed anyone other than family to get as close to me as my young Canadian friends. There was something about this group. You could see it in their eyes, especially in the seriously focused eyes of the team captain. Their mannerisms and keen sense of fair play were impeccable. It was a great honor and privilege to be associated with them.

I had the habit of telling them to "shake it off" when they hurt. At one practice, one of them came sliding home and came up with a bloody nose. Seeing this, I immediately told him to "shake it off," but the poor guy looked up pleading and said "Willie, I can't shake this one off." After a brief trip to the hospital, he was fully recovered. Other than that, there were no injuries that occurred. When the season ended and time came for me to leave Canada, I was pleasantly surprised by a party, hosted by my young Canadian friends, and held at the home of our team captain. It was a happy memorable occasion, and they presented me with several handsome gifts. The team captain remarked, "We hope you come back next year Willie, because you are a great coach." To me that was the supreme compliment. Leaving those young fellows who made the summer of 1951 so special was emotional for me. Mr. Schwab also expressed wishes that I return.

When they played/sang their national anthem "O CANADA", my emotions flowed and chills ran up and down my spine because I sincerely knew that I was an accepted and respected guest in their beloved homeland, a guest who had the opportunity to revisit his friends 43 years later.

I wondered what opportunities would be available upon my return to Carlisle, and also if I would return to Canada next season to coach the team.

CHAPTER 6

Pro-Ball Tryout

BROOKLYN DODGER TRAINING CAMP
Vero Beach, Florida

Friends in Philadelphia had arranged for me to have a tryout with the Brooklyn Dodgers of the National Baseball League. At the time, the Dodgers were the cream of the crop. I arrived at Vero Beach in early February 1952 and was issued a uniform and assigned to specific sleeping quarters at the complex. The training was intense, but after a couple of days there I was in great shape. All the well-known Dodgers were there – Jackie Robinson, Roy Campanella, Don Newcomb, Carl Furillo, Clem Labine, Gil Hodges, Pee Wee Reese, Johnny Padres (pitching coach of the National League Philadelphia Phillies) and a score of others. I had one brief conversation with Jackie. He was the classic example of a major league baseball superstar, one that could execute plays like a well-oiled machine.

I worked out with many of their minor league teams and thought that I had made a favorable impression on the team officials. The velocity on my fastball had increased tremendously, and I was quite accurate getting the ball over the plate. Once again, I pretended that the ball was being thrown through that old tire hung up on my grandfather's garage.

At that time, discrimination existed in Vero Beach. No Blacks were allowed to enter the business establishments. This problem was quickly solved. It seemed the Cubans on the team had freedom to go wherever they wanted, so they invited me to travel with them and keep my mouth shut. Surprisingly, these tactics worked, so I kept my mouth shut.

Baseball training was much like boot camp training in the Army. Things were done in a disciplined manner within carefully designed time limits. Wind sprints, ball speed (i.e., time required to throw the ball from the mound to the plate) and various other aspects of the game were timed.

With a team like the Dodgers having so much talent, I realized that it would be extremely difficult for me and others to catch on with this team. But no matter what, I hung in there and gave it my best shot. Many others gave up and were sent home.

I wrote many letters home to Mom to keep her up-to-date on my progress and to assure her that everything was OK. She was a constant worrier and very protective of her children. The letters home appear at the end of this chapter.

At the Vero Beach complex, there were a vast number of baseball players trying to make the team. They came from all over the country and also places such as Cuba and Puerto Rico. The Cubans were fun to be around. They smoked their big Havana cigars and always seemed to be having a good time. They also were skilled baseball players. I enjoyed the trips to town with them, because they treated me like one of them. They also had money and at times would purchase things for me. I never will forget them. Because of the luxury of living in a country with a continuously warm climate, they played baseball anytime during the year. As a result, they were always in good physical condition and were able to participate in spring training exercises with little effort.

Significant differences exist at the major and minor league levels. The major league consists primarily of veteran baseball players who consistently excel in their various positions on the diamond. The minor leagues consists primarily of baseball players fresh out of college or high school, with a sprinkling of veterans injured and/or on the disabled list who were sent down to the minor league on a temporary basis for rehabilitation. The primary difference between the major and minor leagues is playing ability.

In the major leagues, the players are far superior to their counterparts in the minor league in many ways. They can generally run faster, hit for higher averages, throw a baseball at a higher velocity, and are overall better skilled ball players. Minor league players who put up good numbers are excellent candidates for advancement to the major leagues.

As the training season was coming to a close, the team officials decided which of the players would be assigned to their farm teams and which players would be cut. Unfortunately, I was cut, so I packed my bags and headed back home to Carlisle.

It was a wonderful experience to be in Vero Beach and meet all those famous players. I thought I was good enough, but apparently they did not think so. Later on, I learned I had survived up to the final two cuts. It appeared that a white player and a Cuban player were chosen over me. I gave it my best shot at stardom and came close. To me that was satisfying to know that I had narrowly missed making the team. As the old saying goes, "many are called, but few are chosen."

Returning to Carlisle after having failed the tryout was heart-breaking, but knowing that I gave it my best shot was all that really mattered. Now the search was on for other job markets.

DODGERTOWN, VERO BEACH, FLORIDA

Dear Mom,

I arrived here safely at 9:15AM Wednesday. It is really warm down here. The temperature was around 77° today, so you can see that it is hot. You don't even have to wear a coat.

You can go right out doors and pick an orange or grapefruit right off the tree. The food is swell here and we can get all we want to eat. All the milk we can drink.

I got my uniform today, but I haven't been on the field yet. We are supposed to start training tomorrow. I hope I do well. In the afternoon, I saw the Dodgers playing the Cincinnati Reds. The Dodgers won 3 to 2.

I am going to write Mr. Schwab + Mr. Hurst from down here. You can send my mail down here when it comes for me.

Well I guess I will close for now and when you write you can write to the same address on the paper.

Your son,
"Will"

P.S. - Tell everyone I said hello.

DODGERTOWN, VERO BEACH, FLORIDA

March 26, 1952

Dear "Mom",

Your letter came today. I am well and hope these few lines find you and everyone at home the same.

Well it rained here for the first time since, I have been here. For the past week it has been close to 90° F every day. Down here we don't need to wear many clothes. It really gets hot here.

This food is really good down here and we certainly get enough to eat. I don't think I will be able to send any oranges or grapefruits because they would cost the same as they would up there to send them.

We have played 3 exhibition games so far. We won our 23 to 3, lost the second one 6 to 2 and tied our third game 1 to 1. I pitched three innings of the first game and pitched no hit, shut out ball while I was in the game. Mr. Spait, who is here, said that I looked good.

We really train hard down here. We do a lot of running to get into shape. We also have sliding practise and batting practise. You can imagine how tired we get in the sun practising day after day. There are approximately 300 base ball players here and you can imagine how small one can feel in that vast number.

Mr. Sport asked me if I needed any money to come around and see him. I think I will go around to see him tomorrow. He seems to be very nice and he has had the photographer take some pictures of me. They have sent the box scores of our exhibition games to the Lancaster paper.

I have heard that the Lancaster team will leave around the 17th of April for Lancaster. They are supposed to play some exhibition games up North before the season starts. I think the Inter-State League starts on the 23rd of April.

All of the Minor League teams affiliated with the Dodgers are here at Vero Beach. The "Dodgers" are in Miami now where they will stay until they go up North.

Well I guess I will close for this time. Take care of yourself and tell everyone that I said hello.

Your son,

"Will"

The BROOKLYN Dodgers
AND AFFILIATED CLUBS — SPRING TRAINING CAMP
DODGERTOWN, VERO BEACH, FLORIDA

April 8, 1952

Dear "Mom",

Well I am still here in training at Vero Beach. This sun is really giving me quite a tan, but I am well and hope you & everyone at home are the same.

Since I don't have any insurance on the car, I don't think it will be wise to let "Bunch" use the car. He will understand.

At first for the past two weeks, I had been training with Lancaster and I did pretty good. This week, they have transfered me to the Santa Barbara team which plays in California. If I stay with this team, they will send me to California for the season. That is a long way from Pennsylvania. I hope that I am transfered back to the Lancaster club, but they put us where they want us. This team leaves for California around the 16th of this month.

II

They must think that I can pitch here because if they didn't, they would have sent me home a long time ago. They sent quite a few fellows home.

When we started, there were about 35 negroes here but there are only 20 now. They sent the others home.

Well this will be all for now. Don't worry about my bills. I will send money home just as soon as I start getting paid.

Your son,
"Will"

P.S. Take it easy. Tell everyone I said hello. I will write again soon.

The BROOKLYN Dodgers
AND AFFILIATED CLUBS
SPRING TRAINING CAMP

DODGERTOWN, VERO BEACH, FLORIDA

April 15, 1952

Dear "Mom",

Sorry I didn't get a chance to send any Easter cards home. Just didn't get a chance to get into town to get any. Did Sis have a basket for Jessica? Did Jr. have a basket for Chris?

Tell Jr., just as soon as I start drawing my pay checks, I will send him some money. I don't think I will be playing with Lancaster this year. At the present time, I am on the Hazard, Kentucky team, but I don't know if I will go there or not.

Well how are everyone at home. I am fine. I know I always feel fine as long as there is good food around. (smile)

We will only be here until the 22nd of April and then, we will be assigned to our teams. We don't know where we are going yet.

Everything is swell here. We have free movies here every other night. But, I will be glad when I will be leaving so that I will start drawing that paycheck. We start getting paid after our season starts.

Yes I saw Jackie Robinson, Campanella and all of the other Dodgers. They eat in the same cafeteria as we do. They have started back North now. Their season opens the 15 Th of this month.

At Dodgertown, there is no segregation, but in Vero Beach, there is a lot of that sort of stuff.

Well this will be all for now, but I will write again soon. As soon as I draw my first check, I will send some money home on my bills.

Your son,
Will

P. S. Take it easy and tell everyone I said hello.

CHAPTER 7

Class AA Ball

HARRISBURG SENATORS BASEBALL TEAM
Harrisburg, Pennsylvania (Capital City)

In June of 1952, I joined the Harrisburg Senators Baseball Team of the Eastern League. Harrisburg is about twenty miles east of Carlisle.

Buck Etchinson, a former major league baseball player, was the manager of the Senators. He was very knowledgeable of the game and had the skills to play the game. He also doubled as the Senators' first baseman. I liked him and respected his opinion.

The Senators' home field was City Island Park. The park was beautifully landscaped by a groundskeeper named "Boss Bones". He kept the playing field in superb condition at all times. Many times he could have gone up to the major leagues to manicure their fields, but City Island Park was his love and joy. Boss Bones was a thin wiry man who was always sunburned by the sun. I enjoyed listening to him rattling off stories about his professional associations with big names of the game who had visited City Island Park. He was a heck of a guy.

My mom, grandmom, and brother attended the games and were my best supporters. It was refreshing to look up in the stands and see their happy faces.

My stints on the mound were fairly consistent. I won some and lost some. As always, when I was out there on the mound pitching for the Senators, I could pretend that I was out there throwing the ball through that old tire that hung on my grandfather's garage back in the 1930s.

Since most of the teams we played were located miles away from Harrisburg, the bus trips to and from those games were tiring. However, it was nice to play in their ball parks and visit their surroundings prior to and after the games. The pay was not bad, and we received meal money allowances.

Harrisburg Senators Baseball Team (1952)

What was always foremost in our minds was the fact that we were only two levels under the professional major league level. We realized that with any kind of break, we may have our shot with the majors. Sometimes it is not what you can do that advances you to a higher level, it's generally who you know.

I believed that our manager thought I was good, because he allowed me to start many games and even called me in at times for relief duties. As was the case in Vero Beach, my fast ball had tremendous velocity. Many batters went down on strikes as I whipped that fast ball past them.

Being shy and laid back can be a problem. When you play baseball you must be aggressive with a tremendous desire to win. The desire to win was always there, but I must admit I was very shy. This was probably the result of my earlier years as a young lad living in the country towns of Millerstown and Newport.

My teammates on the Senators were very supportive of me and made many outstanding plays that pulled me out of many jams. I was pleasantly surprised one night to hit a baseball over the City Island Park right field fence. As I rounded third base, I saw my family on their feet, shouting and celebrating my home run. That was one of the highlights of my playing days with the Senators. The other was the night of July 19, 1994 when I was permitted to throw out the first ball prior to the Senators' home game. My emotions flowed. When the announcer called my name, I strolled out to the mound to deliver the pitch. The catcher returned the baseball to me. When I see my Canadian friend (Captain of the 1951 Pee Wee baseball team) again, he will receive that ball as a souvenir of our friendship.

The honor of throwing out the first pitch prior to the start of a game is usually reserved for VIPs (very important persons) and high ranking dignitaries. How I received this honor is beyond my wildest imagination. Perhaps Pam Chavis and my son, Steve, had done something to convince the Senators' team officials to grant that honor. It certainly was nice to receive such a distinction. It is a memory that will last a lifetime.

My First-Pitch Ball during a Harrisburg Senators Game

Part of my boyhood dream of playing professional baseball occurred with the time spent with the Philadelphia teams, Oshawa Merchants, Belleville Redmen, and Harrisburg Senators. I also enjoyed participating in many sandlot baseball games along the way.

The opportunity to play at a higher level class ball never came, but as they say, "It is better to have loved and lost than never to have loved at all." The tryout with the Major

National League Brooklyn Dodgers was the highlight of my professional career.

As stated earlier, baseball provided me the opportunity to meet many people and see many places which I would not have seen. When the National Anthem was played prior to each game, chills ran up and down my spine, and my emotions flowed just as they had during my playing days in Canada when the Canadian National Anthem played.

A new generation of Senators plays at City Island Park (now called Riverside Stadium), and they are a joy to watch. They truly are a consistent, hard-working, championship team. After leaving the Senators' team, I returned to Carlisle and formed a committee of six teenagers at the Carlisle Community Center to encourage young people to become involved in community affairs.

I officiated many athletic contests run by the Carlisle Athletic Association and participated with the "Big Nine", American Legion, and sandlot baseball teams in Carlisle. As my baseball career ended, I still maintained interest in the game. It seems that the games, both at the major and minor levels, are getting longer and longer. In 1990, I sought a patent for a process I developed to be utilized during pitcher warm-up, that I believe would shorten the length of the games. I may not be around to see my process implemented, but I predict that one day it will be used in my beloved game of baseball. (Correspondence with the Commissioner of Baseball concerning this process appears at the end of this Chapter.)

When I returned to Carlisle, I also started a trucking business picking up trash at selected businesses. A young fellow named "Taxi" was my sidekick and really kept busy loading and unloading the items we picked up. He still lives in Carlisle, and even though we do not see each other much, I will never forget how helpful he was to me on our truck runs. He reminded me of my baseball friends in Canada; up early in the morning, hollering "Willie, let's go to work!"

In August 1952, I began employment at the Naval Supply Depot (Ship Parts Control Center/SPCC) in Mechanicsburg, Pennsylvania. The transition from everyday baseball player to a 9-to-5 federal employee wasn't difficult. Even though the long trip to the major league was not completed, it was satisfying and enjoyable to play professional baseball at the "AA" level. While disappointed that I didn't get to the "big show," I knew deep down in my heart that I had given it my best shot, and that was all that really mattered. It was now time to move on to the other job markets and not dwell on what might have been.

Subject: **Baseball Fan's Proposal To Modify:**

PITCHER-CATCHER PRE-INNING WARM-UPS

To: Mr. Francis Vincent / Baseball Commissioner
350 Park Avenue - 17th Floor
New York, New York 10022

From: Mr. Wilbur L. Fordham
3608 Tudor Drive
Harrisburg, Pennsylvania 17109
H: 717-545-7565 - O: 717-234-2022

Date: June 18th, 1990

[A] Current Pitcher-Catcher Pre-Inning Warm-Up Procedure:

Under the current Pitcher-Catcher pre-inning warm-up procedure; prior to the commencement of the first and second halves of each inning; the Pitcher on the mound throws at least eight (8) warm-up pitches to his Catcher, and after each pitch, the Catcher returns (throws the) baseball back to the Pitcher, except for the last pitch by the Pitcher to the Catcher which the Catcher throws to the infielder covering "second-base".

[B] Recommendations for Modification of Pitcher-Catcher Pre-Inning Warm-Up:

During first and second halves of each inning's warm-up periods, eliminate Catcher's return of Baseball to Pitcher...as follows:

(1) Position "Bat-boy" near Pitcher's mound with plastic bucket of baseballs (at least one dozen).

(2) When Pitcher is ready to commence with his warm-up pitches; "bat-boy" would hand Pitcher a baseball from the bucket.

(3) When the Pitcher throws his pre-inning warm-up pitches to his Catcher; the Catcher would merely "catch the ball and throw it to the side and/or in a bucket, and situate himself for the next pitch from his Pitcher.

(4) Because the Pitcher would no longer have to catch a return thrown baseball from his Catcher; the Pitcher is therefore left to fully concentrate on his pitching ability - receiving his balls directly from the "bat-boy" situated near the mound.

-1-

My letter to the Baseball Commissioner
(Pitcher Warm-up Process)

Mr. Francis Vincent
Baseball Commissioner:

-2-

Recommendations for Modification of Pitcher-Catcher Pre-Inning Warm-Up:

(5) Once the Catcher receives his last pitch from his Pitcher; the "bat-boy" is making his way off of the playing field, and gathers up all baseballs disguarded by Catcher, as the Catcher throws his final catch to the Infielder, as "we" get ready to play either that top-half or bottom-half inning.

[C] Immediate & Long Range Benefits from Modified Version:

(1) Permits the Pitcher to fully concentrate on perfecting his pre-inning warm-up pitching skills and ability for regular game performance.

(2) Permits the Catcher to fully concentrate on perfecting his pre-inning warm-up catching skills and ability for regular game performance.

(3) Reduces the existing dangers of either the Pitcher or Catcher from receiving injuries, as a direct result of such pre-inning warm-ups - where the Pitcher may sustain an injury, as a result of attempting to catch a returned thrown baseball from his Catcher, and where the Catcher may sustain an injury in his return throw to the Pitcher.

(4) Eliminates at least 126 pitches from the Catcher to the Pitcher in the course of a normal nine inning game.

(5) Would reduce the wear and tear on both the Pitcher's and Catcher's arm, hence creating the possibility of professional longevity for both.

(6) Would decrease Owner Liability in reference to valued Player Contracts and the expection of their over all professional performances in regular innings and games.

(7) Would fully permit both the Pitcher and Catcher to concentrate on what they are being paid handsomely to perfect: Pitch & Catch.

(8) Woūld speed up regular Baseball Game playing activity.

(9) Would stimulate increased F A N satisfaction, as everyone enjoys changes.

Mr. Francis Vincent
Baseball Commissioner:

-3-

[D] **Chart of Recommended Procedural Change**

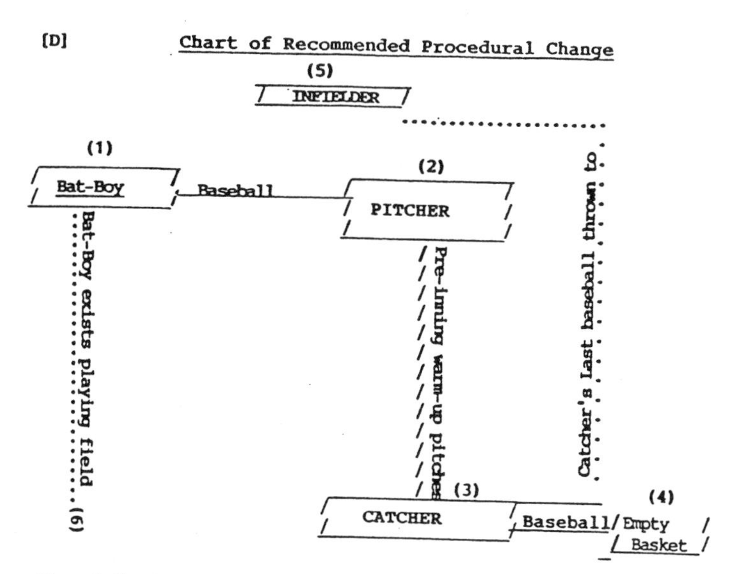

Steps Defined:

(1) Bat-boy hands baseballs to Pitcher
(2) Pitcher throws pre-inning baseballs to his Catcher.
(3) Catcher catches pre-inning pitches
(4) Catcher disregards baseballs to the side and/or in basket.
(5) Catcher throws last baseball from Pitcher to Infielder.
(6) Bat-Boy exits playing field for dug-out.

Wilbur L. Fordham
Wilbur L. Fordham

Sworn to and subscribed before me
LeRoy H. Shirk (Notary Public)
on this 19 day of June, 1990
My Commission expires:

Notarial Seal
LeRoy H. Shirk, Notary Public
Carlisle Boro, Cumberland County
My Commission Expires Aug. 16, 1993

WLF:lhs:cc

FRANCIS T. VINCENT, JR.
Commissioner

September 14, 1990

Mr. Wilbur L. Fordham
3608 Tudor Drive
Harrisburg, PA 17109

Dear Mr. Fordham:

Thank you for your recent letter and for the interest which you have expressed in Major League Baseball. Your comments and ideas regarding the modification of pitcher-catcher warm-up procedures have been duly noted. Your idea is creative, but I am not certain it is necessary or practical.

As I have expressed on many occasions, I believe that baseball occupies a special place in American life. Consequently, I am always interested in knowing the views of the fans whose devotion to the game has made it a national institution.

Sincerely,

Fay Vincent

Francis T. Vincent, Jr.

FTV:djb

350 Park Avenue, New York, N.Y. 10022 (212) 339-7815

Letter from Mr. Francis Vincent, Jr.
(Baseball Commissioner)

Wilbur L. Fordham
3608 Tudor Drive
Harrisburg, PA 17109

November 11, 1990

To: Mr. Francis T. Vincent, Jr. , Commissioner of Major League Baseball

From: Wilbur L. Fordham

Subj: PITCHER-CATCHER PRE-INNING WARM-UP PROPOSAL; RESPONSE

Ref: (a) Pitcher-Catcher Pre-inning Warm-up proposal dated June 18, 1990

(b) Office of the Commissioner of Major League Baseball letter dated September 14, 1990

Dear Mr. Vincent:

I would like to thank you for responding to my proposal submitted to your office in reference (a). In your response forwarded to me in reference (b), you stated that my "comments and ideas regarding the modification of pitcher-catcher warm-up procedures have been duly noted". You also stated that you were not "certain" if my idea was necessary or practical. Reading your comments, I am not sure at this point if you would still give my proposal consideration for future possibilities. I strongly believe that my idea would benefit baseball in the various ways mentioned in reference (a), and have sought legal (patent) protection for my proposal. I request that if my idea is given consideration for trial or implementation in either the major or minor league systems, that I be notified so that any necessary arrangements can be worked out between myself and your organization.

My follow-up letter to the Commissioner

My follow-up letter to the Commissioner (cont.)

As I had stated in my previous letter, I am not only a former minor league pitcher (Harrisburg Senators) but also a devoted fan, and that is why I know my idea explained in my proposal can make the great game of baseball even better. I want to thank you for your time Mr. Vincent, and I hope to hear from you concerning your intentions for the use of my concept.

Sincerely,

Wilbur L. Fordham

Wilbur L. Fordham

cc: Litman Law Offices

File

FRANCIS T. VINCENT, JR.
Commissioner

January 23, 1991

Mr. Wilbur L. Fordham
3608 Tudor Drive
Harrisburg, PA 17109

Dear Mr. Fordham:

Thank you for your follow-up letter and for your continued interest in Major League Baseball. At this time, however, our office does not intend to implement your idea in Major League Baseball.

Sincerely,

Fay Vincent

Francis T. Vincent, Jr.

FTV:irk

350 Park Avenue, New York, N.Y. 10022 (212)339-7800

The Commissioner's second letter of reply

CHAPTER 8

Job and Family Living

FEDERAL GOVERNMENT EMPLOYMENT
Mechanicsburg, Pennsylvania
&
CALDER STREET
1421 Calder Street,
Harrisburg, Pennsylvania

On August 4, 1952, I began working for the Federal Government at the Naval Supply Depot located in Mechanicsburg. It is approximately twenty miles from Harrisburg where I now reside. The Depot's primary function is supplying to the United States Navy, a Navy second to none.

I began work at Mechanicsburg as a supply clerk and later advanced to the position of Supply System Analyst (GS-12).

During my tenure of duty at Mechanicsburg, I made many field trips to various military installations. Some to attend meetings, others to coordinate development of supply system instructions, directives, and so forth. I also had the opportunity to serve on many committees at the base, often as Chairperson. Working at Mechanicsburg enabled me to see many places that I would not have seen or visited.

Many of the projects I worked on at the base were of confidential nature. Some entailed the development of instructions/procedures for complying with tasks assigned by higher authority. Some involved the coordination of meetings with various divisions throughout SPCC. Tasks assigned to me were challenging and the research required to complete them was laborious. Some projects required complex coordination with others to complete, and each project had an established deadline for completion.

The base offered many excellent dining facilities, such as the Executive Room and the Commissioned Officer's Mess. Medical facilities were also available. The base was a city within itself and I enjoyed working there. There was a friendly atmosphere there and all employees were industrious. Reserved parking was available for high echelon personnel (GS-12 and above). Luckily, I had a reserved parking space.

While working in Mechanicsburg, I was fortunate to meet many good people who still remain in touch. One former fellow employee always makes sure that my family receives vegetables from his garden each year. His name is Fred Kozak, and he lives in Marysville, PA with his wife, Betty. Another person is Bob Goshorn who makes sure that my family gets delicious pecans from Florida.

Paul Ruth helped me tremendously during my federal service career. I can recall a time when he considered me for advancement to a management position. He went to the Admiral stating that he was contemplating placing the first black man in a management position. The Admiral's reply was, "I don't care if he is blue or pink; can he do the job?" Paul and I often got a big kick over that incident. Armed Forces Day was held each year at the Depot and was always exciting, as were the big picnics hosted by the Supervisor's Association. I was in charge of many of the athletic contests at these picnics. Paul's wife, Lillian, won most of these contests. I called her superwoman.

The Mechanicsburg Supply Depot is also where I met my wife, the former Jessie Caroline Fountain.

I worked at Mechanicsburg for 30 years and retired on July 16, 1982. Retirement parties were very ceremonial and afforded an opportunity to salute the retirees. I figured that I didn't have a party when I came, so there was no necessity for one when I left.

Navy Ships Parts Control Center

This is to certify that

WILBUR L. FORDHAM

completed 30 years of Federal Service on the

19th day of August 1980

This certificate is awarded as a Testimonial of

Faithful and Honorable Service

U S Navy

Retirement Certificate

The salaries that Jessie and I earned at the Depot paved the way for purchase of our first home at 1421 Calder Street in Harrisburg. Our three sons were raised there. My brother-in-law, James Fountain, Jr., and I spent many a day and evening preparing the backyard for a swimming pool, which was used constantly by my sons and all their friends. It was quite a project that really paid off.

Working long hours and coming home to Calder Street from the depot would sometimes present us with problems. One day, our youngest son, Byron, was lying on the porch with a big gash in his leg. It was the result of a weird accident. I never will forget how shook up my wife was. We took him to the hospital to get stitches, but the harrowing experience of seeing our son with a gaping 10 to 12 inch wound was almost too much to handle. Unfortunately, the wound healed on the surface but not underneath. So, it busted open again while Byron was playing baseball, and he had to be treated by a surgeon for six weeks before it healed properly. Byron still has the scar to remind us of this experience.

Overall, life on Calder Street was peaceful, much like the atmosphere in Millerstown and Newport. We had many friends and enjoyed many parties there. All the neighborhood children played together and people generally looked out for one another.

Thanks to our jobs at the depot, we were able to live comfortably and raise our children in a relatively safe environment. They enjoyed Calder Street and often remarked how much fun they were having there, especially during the holiday seasons when I would take them on sled rides.

After living on Calder Street for seventeen years, my family moved to reside in our current house that we had built in Susquehanna Township in 1972. As a result of my wife's diligent efforts of putting money with the monthly mortgage payments, the mortgage on our home in Susquehanna Township was paid off prior to the maturity date. At our mortgage burning party, in August of 1993, many relatives and friends from far and near came to help us celebrate our accomplishment of that awesome task. We take pride and joy in the ownership of our home. Our home is located in Oxford Court, a community comprised of over 100 homes. It is close to many malls and major interstate highways.

As mentioned earlier, I owned and operated a T.V. repair shop in Harrisburg with my uncle Jim. We named our business "Greenford TV", however it is affectionately known as "The Shop."

Our house on Tudor Drive

CHAPTER 9

The Shop

GREENFORD TV
343 Peffer Street
Harrisburg, Pennsylvania

On August 3, 1963, my uncle Jim, (the same person I grew up with in Millerstown) and I opened Greenford TV Sales and Service store. The name was a combination of sorts– GREEN being his last name and FORD being the first part of my last name. Jim resides in Harrisburg with his wife, Margaret. Their children are Gwendolyn and Gregory who reside in Harrisburg, Dr. Wendy of California, and Carmen of Tennessee.

Initially, our minority owned business was operated on a part-time basis, because we both worked at the Mechanicsburg Navy Supply Depot. During the first years of operation, we built a steady clientele. We purchased a van to handle delivery/pickup of electronic items. My Uncle Jim ran the service department, and I took care of business transactions and sales. This arrangement was quite satisfactory.

Our motto was and still is "Our Aim Is To Please Our Customers," and we honestly tried to do just that.

Being in the shop each evening and all day Saturday sometimes prevented me from spending quality time with my sons. Every now and then, my wife will mention the fact that she often wished that I was around more to help with raising our sons. I always believed that they knew how much I loved and cared for them, and that Dad was out there making a buck to pay the bills and keep a roof over their heads. However, at an early age, Son Steve worked in the shop answering the phone and performing general clean-up tasks. He also engaged in sales talks with potential customers. He was an integral part of the Greenford TV operation.

Many friends have purchased items from our business even though they may have gotten a better deal elsewhere. To them I will be forever grateful. These are the customers who have kept us in business over the past 35 years.

At times we had new televisions, radios, and stereo equipment on display. These items, when purchased by our customers, would be financed through a local bank. However, the store is located in a distressed area of the city, and never reached the full potential we anticipated.

We had many break-ins at the shop, some resulting in loss of equipment and electronic items such as television sets, radios, etc. Numerous windows had to be replaced and new doors installed. Because of the frequent break-ins, we no longer have merchandise on display in the store. However, customer needs for new electronic products are satisfied by our business purchasing these products from selected distributors. Most electronic parts needed to service television sets are attainable through our local electronic wholesalers. We were disheartened by the break-ins, but it never diminished our desires to remain in business and provide for those customers that needed us the most.

The business at times was nerve-wracking, but we

hung in there because we knew the community was in need of our services. Some customers don't pay their bills and others fail to pick up their items even after being advised they are ready for pickup. As a result, cash flow was reduced and intermittent.

Being at the same location for 35 years has had its rewards. I have met a lot of people involved in the television business who have been helpful to me and I like to think that maybe I was of some help to them also. Dick Bushman and Les Hines have been in the television business for many years and have helped me tremendously. They have certainly gone the extra mile for me on many occasions, and their efforts are greatly appreciated.

My uncle Jim departed the business many years ago and I, after retiring from the depot in 1982, continued operations there on a full-time basis until I started employment with the Commonwealth of Pennsylvania.

After 35 years, Greenford TV is planning to shut down, primarily due to my health problems that prevent me from doing the tasks I used to do. It is comforting to know that Greenford TV satisfied a community need over the years through its sales/service operations. The good customers acquired over the years remained faithful. Without them the business would have failed.

What to do in the future is a sticky situation; get another job, vacation, or simply relax at home? Being active all my life and suddenly retreating to a life of relaxation is scary. My family's concerns are most important and will influence the future course of action I will follow.

It was one heck of a ride being the owner of Greenford TV, one of which I am extremely proud. No one knows what will happen in the future, but hopefully the best is yet to come.

CHAPTER 10

Kudos

ARTICLES/LETTERS OF APPRECIATION

As a result of the sole efforts of Pam Chavis and our son, Steve, public airing of my life story appeared in a Harrisburg Patriot-News article. Letters of praise for my accomplishments were received from several prominent professional leaders/organizations. The newspaper articles and letters of praise appear on the following pages. These honors and recognitions made me fully realize that even though "I gave it my best shot" and didn't make it to the big leagues, I was appreciated by my family, friends, and the community. To be honest, I was deeply humbled by the enormity of these kind kudos. Fortunately, I never let success go to my head (entirely), and defeat did not destroy my ambition to succeed.

As I explained earlier in my introductory remarks, positively never ever give up. The same types of blessings that I have received may come your way as long as you keep your eye on the prize and GIVE IT YOUR BEST SHOT!

Metro East

TUESDAY
July 12, 1994
The Patriot-News
Harrisburg, Pa.

Summer of '52

For The Patriot-News/Norman Arnold

HIS FIELD OF DREAMS — AND MEMORIES — Fordham looks over Riverside.

Ex-Senator recalls heyday on the mound

By Bernie Mixon
Patriot-News

He could feel the adrenaline surge, the ball in his hand, the cap on his head. Standing on the pitcher's mound at Harrisburg's Riverside Stadium, he could almost hear the crowd roar.

Sights and sounds of a time gone by, a time when he carved out his own field of dreams as a pitcher with the 1952 Harrisburg Senators. A moment when the handsome young man from Carlisle, with a smile as lethal as his killer fastball, ruled the mound.

His Riverside visit last week was

See MEMORIES — Page 18

Patriot-News Article (July 12, 1994)

Patriot-News Article (cont.)

18—Metro East, July 12, 1994

AROUND THE REGION

Ex-Senator returns to his glory days on the mound

MEMORIES — From Page 1

the first time that Wilbur Fordham, now 67, had been back on the field where a new generation of Senators play. He spent time in the stands, on the mound, in the dugout, taking it all in.

"It brought back memories," said Fordham, now of Susquehanna Twp. who will be honored by his friends and family on Saturday for his accomplishments on the baseball field and off.

"My emotions flowed," he said. "It brought back the days when I was out there pitching and socializing with the other players and fans."

Fordham's love for America's pastime began as a young boy in Millerstown, when he would pitch balls through an old tire hung from his grandfather's garage, all the while dreaming of becoming a professional baseball player.

The family moved from Millerstown to Newport and settled in Carlisle, where Fordham pitched for the high school team. While there, he pitched a no-hitter during his perfect season and excelled in other sports such as track and basketball.

Following high school, he was drafted into the Army, and, two years later, he enrolled at Cheyney Teacher's College. Cheyney didn't have a baseball team, but he played in a Philadelphia league to earn extra money on the weekends.

After he graduated from college, he went to Canada to play with the Oshawa Merchants and the Belleville Redmen, both professional teams. But it wasn't all business for Fordham.

"It gave me the chance to meet different people, observe different customs," he said.

He even found time to coach a Canadian pee-wee baseball team called the Belleville Schwabs. Once the season ended, the sponsor of the Schwabs offered Fordham a job but he declined because he had something bigger than pee-wee in mind: He'd been invited to try out for the Brooklyn Dodgers in Vero Beach, Fla.

Once there, he was playing besides some of baseball's greats — Hall of Famer Jackie Robinson, Roy Campanella, Newt Newcomb, Carl Furillo, Gil Hodges, Johnny Padre and others.

"Just a rookie," Fordham said, so he didn't spend too much time with his heroes away from the diamond during his two month tryout. "I was very shy and laid back. But it was a wonderful experience."

Not all his experiences, however, were that wonderful. "In Vero Beach at that time, no blacks were allowed to go into the stores," he said. "But the Cubans could, so they said for me to go along with them. I went along and didn't open my mouth."

He gave stardom his best shot, but it was not to be. Fordham didn't make the cut, a decision that he accepted even if he didn't agree. "The Dodgers were the cream of the crop," he said. "I thought I was good enough but they didn't think so."

So he returned to Carlisle and joined the Harrisburg Senators in 1952 as a pitcher. Andy Musser, who calls games for the Philadelpia Phillies, was a bat-boy then for the Senators.

"I had a fair record," Ford-

Patriot-News Article (cont.)

ham said of his stint with the Senators. "Won some and lost some." At the end of that season, the team dissolved.

So then he played sandlot ball with the Carlisle Legion Baseball Team and started a sports program for youth in Carlisle.

But as the door closed on his baseball career, another opened. In 1952, he began as a systems analyst in the planning division for the Navy Ship Parts Control Center in Hampden Two. He retired in 1982.

There he met his future wife, the former Jessie Carolyn Fountain, and the couple had three sons, Stephen, Daniel and Byron.

Three years later, Fordham TV Sales and Service began in the basement of his Calder Street home. Fordham formed a partnership with his uncle, James Green, to open Greenford's TV Sales and Service at 343 Peffer St.

Business was good in the 1960s and 1970s, but crime began to escalate and the business was racked by a series of robberies. Windows in the store have been shot out as well.

Still he never considered moving his store. It has served as a meeting place for people in the neighborhood, a "watering hole," his wife says.

In the last five years, the business has not had too many robberies, Fordham said. There is sort of a code of honor among thieves that his shop is off-limits, his friends say. "I think they know I'm a part of the community," Fordham said."

"The kids like him," Mrs. Fordham said. "He has a good rapport with people and is very sensitive. You knew you could always count on him and he was always supportive of young people."

Time is passing, and Fordham hopes to turn his business over to his son one day. But Wilbur Fordham doesn't want anyone to cry for him. He has lived a good life, he said.

"I got the chance to meet a lot of people and saw places that I wouldn't have if it were not for baseball," he said. "I have been blessed."

Commonwealth of Pennsylvania

Governor's Office

TO: WILBUR LEWIS FORDHAM

I am delighted to extend warmest wishes to you as you gather with family and friends to celebrate your 67th birthday.

Your lifetime has yielded an impressive array of varied achievements, from your success as a young athlete in Carlisle to the continuing success of the business which you have operated for 31 years in Harrisburg. In addition, you dutifully served in the United States Army, played professional baseball with the Harrisburg Senators and others, and have given 35 years of dedicated service as a systems analyst with the U.S. Navy Ships Parts Control Center in Mechanicsburg. Through your many activities and accomplishments, you have truly earned the respect and admiration of all who know you, and you can take pride in a job well done.

Happy Birthday, and best wishes for many more years of happiness and success.

Robert P. Casey
Governor
July 15, 1994

Letter from Governor of Pennsylvania (Gov. Robert P. Casey)

Office of The Mayor

Harrisburg, Pennsylvania

Proclamation

WHEREAS,

Amongst this region's most-respected and admired native sons is the inimitable Wilbur Lewis Fordham, who on this the 67th anniversary of his birth is being honored by family, friends and admirers for a lifetime of accomplishment and good will; and

WHEREAS,

Married to the former Jessie Carolyn Fountain and the father of sons Stephen Blaine, Daniel Lamont and Byron Lewis Fordham; this dynamic young man performed admirable public service as a systems analyst for 35 years at the Navy Ships Parts Control Center as well as a private community retailer at Greenfords TV Sales and Service at 328 Peffer St.; and

WHEREAS,

A respected and honored Army veteran, Wilbur was educated at Cheyney State Teacher's College and a member of the distinguished Alpha Phi Alpha Fraternity; and

WHEREAS,

An outstanding student athlete who led his Carlisle High School baseball team to an 8-0 record, Wilbur went on to achieve significant fame with the Oshawa Merchants and the Belleville Redmon Baseball Team in Canada, as well as a tryout with the then Brooklyn Dodgers, where he played along side such legends as Jackie Robinson, Roy Campanella, and Gil Hodges, and with the original Harrisburg Senators during the 1952-53 baseball season; and

WHEREAS,

It is appropriate and warranted that such a dynamic athlete, father and husband, public servant and community role model be duly honored and feted; now therefore be it hereby designated and

PROCLAIMED

That Saturday, July 16, 1994, be declared

WILBUR LEWIS FORDHAM DAY

In and for the citizens of the City of Harrisburg, Capital of the Commonwealth of Pennsylvania, with all citizens urged to recognize and appreciate the many contributions this outstanding young man has made to our community and Nation.

SET UNDER MY HAND AND SEAL THIS SEVENTH DAY OF JULY, NINETEEN HUNDRED AND NINETY-FOUR

Stephen R. Reed

MAYOR STEPHEN R. REED

Proclamation from Mayor of Harrisburg, Pennsylvania (Mayor Stephen R. Reed)

Office Of City Council
Harrisburg, Pennsylvania

Resolution

I offer the following Resolution and move its adoption:

WHEREAS, Wilbur Lewis Fordham, is a lifelong resident of South Central Pennsylvania; and

WHEREAS, excelling at Carlisle High School as a pitcher, he played professional baseball at age 21 in Canada with the Oshawa Merchants and the Belleville Redman Baseball teams; and

WHEREAS, in 1952, Mr. Fordham tried out as a pitcher with the Brooklyn Dodgers, alongside Jackie Robinson, Roy Campanella, and Gil Hodges among others; and

WHEREAS, he did not play for the Brooklyn Dodgers, but was selected as a pitcher for the Harrisburg Senators Baseball Team during the 1952-1953 season; and

WHEREAS, after his professional baseball career ended, Mr. Fordham began an illustrious career as a coach and motivator of young people influencing many youth in uptown Harrisburg.

NOW, THEREFORE, BE AND IT IS HEREBY RESOLVED THAT HARRISBURG CITY COUNCIL commends Wilbur Lewis Fordham on both the quality of his life and the thousands of young people he touched as an athlete, coach and community leader.

BE IT FURTHER RESOLVED THAT CITY COUNCIL joins the celebration of his 67th birthday and declares July 16, 1994 as Wilbur Lewis Fordham day in the City of Harrisburg.

CITY CLERK

Resolution from Harrisburg City Council

Commonwealth of Pennsylvania

Pennsylvania Legislative

Black Caucus

CITATION

Whereas, Wilbur Lewis Fordham, is being honored by his family, friends, and colleagues in commemoration of his 67th birthday on July, 16, 1994; and,

Whereas, Wilbur Fordham served in the U.S. Army, and is retired from the Federal Government after 35 years as a systems analyst at the Navy Ship Parts Control Center in Mechanicsburg. Wilbur Fordham is married to the former Jessie Carolyn Fountain, and has three sons; Stephen, Daniel, and Byron Fordham.

Now therefore, be it resolved that the Pennsylvania Legislative Black Caucus wishes to congratulate Wilbur Lewis Fordham in recognition of his 67th birthday, and bestow best wishes upon him in all his future endeavors.

And directs, that a copy of this citation be delivered to our brother Wilbur Lewis Fordham, at 3608 Tudor Drive in Susquehanna Township, Harrisburg, PA.

Sponsors: Vincent Hughes

REP. VINCENT HUGHES
CHAIRMAN

Citation from Commonwealth of Pennsylvania Legislative Black Caucus

Senate of Pennsylvania

HARRISBURG, PA.

Congratulations

In the Senate, June 28, 1994

Whereas, Wilbur Lewis Fordham is being honored upon the momentous occasion of his sixty-seventh birthday for his lifetime achievements and outstanding contributions to all those who have lived, served and worked with him; and

Whereas, A stellar athlete at Carlisle High School, Mr. Fordham garnered an exceptional career record in baseball. In his senior year, he pitched a no-hitter and had an undefeated pitching record of eight wins and zero losses; and

Whereas, A veteran of the United States Army, Mr. Fordham graduated from Cheyney State Teacher's College. After thirty-five years of dedicated service, he retired from the federal government as a systems analyst in the planning division at the Navy Ship Parts Control Center. Mr. Fordham is also the co-owner of Greenford's TV Sales and Service, a home entertainment and appliance business which has been in existence since 1958.

Now therefore, the Senate of the Commonwealth of Pennsylvania congratulates Wilbur Lewis Fordham on his richly deserved recognition; commends him for being a great benefactor of the community in the finest American tradition; offers best wishes for every future happiness and success;

And directs that a copy of this document, sponsored by Senator John J. Shumaker, be transmitted to Wilbur Lewis Fordham, 3608 Tudor Drive, Harrisburg, Pennsylvania.

Attest: [signature]

Mark R. Corrigan, Secretary

Congratulations from the Commonwealth of Pennsylvania Senate

AFRICAN-AMERICAN
CHAMBER OF COMMERCE

July 15, 1994

Mr. Wilbur Lewis Fordham
3608 Tudor Drive
Harrisburg, Pennsylvania 17110

Dear Mr. Fordham:

The African-American Chamber of Commerce, an advocate organization for African-American Businesses, joins with your family, friends, and colleagues in wishing you a happy 67th birthday.

Moreover, the African-American Chamber of Commerce joins with all of Central Pennsylvania in applauding your lifetime of achievement and accomplishments. Particularly, the Chamber commends you for your business, Greenford's TV Sales and Service, which has thrived in the City of Harrisburg for thirty-one (31) years.

On behalf of the Board of Directors and members of the African-American Chamber of Commerce, I wish you continued success with your business, and, may God bless you and your family.

Sincerely,

William F. Peterson
Executive Director

African-American Chamber of Commerce

Commissioners
President
Stanley R. Lawson, Sr.
Vice President
Robert J. Altoff

Jack Solomon
Michael R. Pender
Steven J. Condes
George H. Searight
Nancy G. Allen
A. Robert Mendelsohn
Jesse Rawls

SUSQUEHANNA TOWNSHIP

Officers
Secretary-Manager
Miles A. Caughey, P.E.
Solicitor
John A. Roe, Esq.
107 North Front Street
Harrisburg, PA 17101
Engineer
Robert C. Grubic, P.E.
Herbert, Rowland & Grubic
369 East Park Drive
Harrisburg, PA 17111

NINETEEN HUNDRED LINGLESTOWN ROAD, HARRISBURG, PENNSYLVANIA 17110 (717) 545-4751
FAX 652-5628

PRESIDENTIAL PROCLAMATION

FOR:

WILBUR LEWIS FORDHAM

WHEREAS, Wilbur Lewis Fordham, who resides at 3608 Tudor Drive in Susquehanna Township, Harrisburg, Pa., is being honored by his family, friends, and colleagues in commemoration of his 67th birthday on July 16, 1994; and

WHEREAS, Wilbur Lewis Fordham was an outstanding athlete at Carlisle High School where in his senior year he pitched a no-hitter and had an undefeated pitching record of 8-0; and

WHEREAS, Wilbur Lewis Fordham served in the U.S. Army and was honorably discharged in 1947 at which time he enrolled in Cheyney State Teacher's College where he received his Bachelor of Science Degree and was a member of the Alpha Phi Alpha Fraternity; and;

WHEREAS, Wilbur Lewis Fordham at age 21, played professional baseball with the Oshawa Merchants and the Belleville Redman Baseball Team in Canada where he also coached the Schwab Peewee Baseball Team; and

Susquehanna Township Council

Susquehanna Township Council (cont.)

WHEREAS, Wilbur Lewis Fordham later was invited to try out with the Brooklyn Dodgers in Vero Beach, Florida where he played alongside baseball great such as Jackie Robinson, Roy Campanili, Newt Newcomb, Carl Furillo, Gil Hodges, Don Labin, Johnny Padre, and others; and

WHEREAS, Wilbur Lewis Fordham later joined the Harrisburg Senators Professional Baseball Team as a pitcher for the 1952-1953 baseball season and later played sandlot baseball with the Carlisle Legion Baseball Team; and

WHEREAS, Wilbur Lewis Fordham retired from the federal government after 35 years as a systems analyst in the planning division at the Navy Ship Parts Control Center in Mechanicsburg; and

WHEREAS, Wilbur Lewis Fordham started a home entertainment and appliance business in his home in 1958 and in 1963, along with his uncle, James Green, opened Greenford's TV Sales and Service at 328 Peffer Street and that business has thrived in the City of Harrisburg for 31 years; and

WHEREAS, Wilbur Lewis Fordham is married to the former Jessie Carolyn Fountain and raised three sons, Stephen Blaine, Daniel Lamont, and Bryon Lewis Fordham;

NOW therefore, let it be resolved that the Susquehanna Township Board of Commissioners joins with all of Central Pennsylvania in applauding this beneficent native son for his lifetime of achievement and accomplishments.

Miles A. Caughey
Secretary-Manager

Stanley R. Lawson, Sr.
President

The President
Cheyney University of Pennsylvania
Cheyney, Pennsylvania 19319
[illegible]

7/15/94

Mr. Wilbur L. Fordham
3608 Tudor Drive
Harrisburg, PA 17102

Dear Mr. Fordham:

On behalf of the Cheyney University family of students, faculty, staff and alumni, it is my honor to wish you a happy 67th birthday, and to congratulate you for a lifetime of accomplishments.

We want you to know that Cheyney University, your alma mater, has not forgotten you or your accomplishments during your time here as a member of the University choir and Alpha Phi Alpha Fraternity. This is especially pleasant for me because I am a member of the same fraternity.

Your family at Cheyney applauds you for your achievements since graduating in 1949. You have provided an exemplary example of all that is positive for our youth to emulate.

Sincerely,

Douglas Covington, Ph.D.
President

State System of Higher Education • Commonwealth of Pennsylvania

Cheyney University
(I actually graduated in 1951)

Proclamation For: Wilbur Lewis Fordham

WHEREAS, Wilbur Lewis Fordham, who resides at 3608 Tudor Drive in Susquehanna Township, Harrisburg, PA, is being honored by his family, friends, and colleagues in commemoration of his 67th birthday on July 16, 1994; and

WHEREAS, Wilbur Lewis Fordham was an outstanding athlete at Carlisle High School where in his senior year he pitched a no-hitter an had an undefeated pitching record of 8-0; and

WHEREAS, Wilbur Lewis Fordham served in the U.S. Army and was honorably discharged in 1947 at which time he enrolled in Cheyney State Teacher's College where he received his Bachelor of Science Degree and was a member of the Alpha Phi Alpha Fraternity; and

WHEREAS, Wilbur Lewis Fordham at age 21, played professional baseball with the Oshawa Merchants and the Belleville Redman Baseball Team in Canada where he also coached the Schwab Peewee Baseball Team; and

WHEREAS, Wilbur Lewis Fordham later was invited to try out with the Brooklyn Dodgers in Vero Beach, Florida where he played alongside baseball greats such as Jackie Robinson, Roy Campanella, Newt Newcomb, Carl Furillo, Gil Hodges, Don Labin, Johnny Padre, and others; and

HARRISBURG SENATORS BASEBALL CLUB
P.O. Box 15757 Harrisburg, PA 17105 717-231-4444

Harrisburg Senators Baseball Team

Harrisburg Senators Baseball Team (continued)

WHEREAS, Wilbur Lewis Fordham later joined the Harrisburg Senators Professional Baseball Team as a pitcher for the 1952-1953 baseball seasons and later played sandlot baseball with the Carlisle Legion Baseball Team; and

WHEREAS, Wilbur Lewis Fordham retired from the federal government after 35 years as a systems analyst in the planning division at the Navy Ship Parts Control Center in Mechanicsburg; and

WHEREAS, Wilbur Lewis Fordham started a home entertainment and appliance business in his home in 1958 and in 1963, along with his uncle, James Green, opened Greenford's TV Sales and Service at 328 Peffer Street and that business has thrived in the City of Harrisburg for 31 years; and

WHEREAS, Wilbur Lewis Fordham is married to the former Jessie Carolyn Fountain and raised three sons, Stephen Blaine, Daniel Lamont, and Byron Lewis Fordham;

NOW THEREFORE, let it be resolved that THE HARRISBURG SENATORS BASEBALL CLUB joins with all of Central Pennsylvania in applauding this beneficient native son for his lifetime of achievement and accomplishment.

HARRISBURG SENATORS BASEBALL CLUB
P.O. Box 15757 Harrisburg, PA 17105 717-231-4444

Ted Knorr

I am flattered and gratified that Mr. Fordham, Willie, asked me to write a brief supplement to the second printing of his book. As I have found out on the lecture circuit, Willie is an inspirational speaker and a true role model for our youth. Everywhere that I have seen him appear he is the star of the show; with kids and adults gathering around him to hear his stories of life and baseball. The last professional team that Willie Fordham played on was the Harrisburg Giants in 1954. Since I both revere and chronicle this team and its predecessors, Willie asked me to write a few words about them.

The Harrisburg Giants took their name from a proud baseball franchise that was founded in Harrisburg in 1890 by local African-American entrepreneur Colonel William Strothers. They competed against all-comers until Strothers death in 1933. They reached their apex in 1925 when they were one of the best baseball teams ANYWHERE IN ANY LEAGUE. That year they finished second to the Hilldale Club of the Eastern Colored League. The Hilldales went on to beat the Kansas City Monarchs, champions of the Negro National League, in the Negro World Series that year. So it should be clear that the Giants were no slouches. In '25, the Giants were led by their playing manager and National Baseball Hall of Famer Oscar Charleston. In addition, the team featured Negro League immortals Ben Taylor, Rap Dixon, Fats Jenkins, Rev. Cannady and Bunny Downs. Earlier, in 1906-08 the great Spottswood Poles and later in 1926-27 John Beckwith also played with the Giants. At their height, the Harrisburg Giants were a major league caliber team – particularly from the offensive side. After Strothers' death the team disbanded and the name went unused for many years.

Meanwhile organized baseball officially reintegrated in 1945 when Jackie Robinson signed a contract with Branch Rickey's Brooklyn Dodgers. In 1946, Jackie reported to Montreal in the International League and in 1947 he joined the big league Dodgers. This marked the beginning of a new era in organized ball and the beginning of an end to an era for an exciting brand of baseball known as the "Negro Leagues".

In 1947, there were still two Negro Leagues, National and American, and an All-Star Game and a World Series. However, by 1950, only one league – the Negro American League – still operated. By 1954, the Negro American League was down to only six teams. In addition to the Negro American League, there existed other leagues that consisted primarily of African-American baseball players. One such league was the Eastern Negro League (ENL).

At about the same time, the great Spottswood Poles who played for the original Harrisburg Colored Giants in one of their heydays from 1906 through 1908 organized and managed a great African-American sandlot team in Harrisburg that he named after his former team – the Harrisburg Giants. Willie Fordham played on the Mr. Poles' Giants in 1953. In 1954, a local hotelier named Rich Felton took over the administrative duties as owner and Tommy Williams replaced the venerable Poles as manager. Two other significant changes occurred on the Giants. First, they joined the Eastern Negro League and second, despite the leagues name, they integrated the team picking up several white players to fill out a roster to compete with the Pittsburgh Crawfords, the Jersey City Giants, Wilmington, Havre de Grace and other ENL squads.

Willie Fordham was one of the star pitchers on the Giants. In addition, according to box scores that I have scanned, he hit .400. In 1954, the Giants were awarded the Doc Marshall Memorial Trophy for winning the ENL's Northern Division. Also on the Giants were two teammates of Willies – the Captain, Tom Hailey and Russ "Rooster Oyster Ram" Royster – from the 1952 edition of the Harrisburg Senators of the Interstate League. Hailey's season long stellar play was recognized by the Gruen Watch Company that presented him with a fine timepiece emblematic of his being named ENL Most Valuable Player. Royster had been signed by the Cleveland Indians just prior to his military service in Korea. The trio was among the first African-Americans to play for the Senators. Other players on the Giants with minor league experience were Ken Freeland and George Kilraine.

1954 Eastern Negro League Northern Division
Final Standings

	W	L	PCT	G.B.
Harrisburg Giants	16	6	.727	—
Pittsburgh Crawfords	14	7	.667	1 1/2
Wilmington Flashes	7	5	.583	4
New York Stars	6	5	.545	4 1/2
Havre de Grace Braves	3	3	.500	5
Newark Giants	3	5	.375	6
Jersey City Cardinals	2	7	.222	7 1/2
Brooklyn Royal Giants	0	13	.000	11 1/2

The Giants won their season opener at Island Park in Harrisburg by a 7-3 score behind Royster. Approximately 1,500 fans attended the game. The season turned in a rain abbreviated scheduled double header on the 5th of July versus the 1st place Pittsburgh Crawfords, the Giants squeezed out a

9-8 victory marking their first success against the Crawfords after three straight defeats during that season. On July 19, Willie Fordham started against Shamokin in a non-league affair won by the Giants 7-6. Other great players on the Giants included pitchers: Thea Dillon, Eddie Nork, Ellwood Harrell, and Danny Werner; catchers: John Peters and Peter "Tomato" Dickey; infielders: Don Ward, Dave McWhite, Reid Poles, Leo "Sike" Burnette, Ezell "Zeke" Jones, Joe Reilly, Vince Hoch, Bruno DiMartile, Bobby Pae, G.G. Burton; outfielders: Jim Weedon, Willie Mims, and Tony Natale. These great heroes were honored at the Harrisburg Senators 3rd annual Negro League Night in July, 1999. Now each year the surviving members are invited back to the site of their glory years, then known as Island Park, which was home in 1890 to the original Harrisburg Giants and under its current appellation, RiverSide Stadium, is home to today's Harrisburg Senators.

Special thanks to Messrs. Fordham, Hailey, Royster, Weedon, Jones and Freeland for their stories of playing on the Doc Marshall Memorial Trophy winning Harrisburg Giants.

Ted Knorr is a local Harrisburg baseball fan and a member of the Society for American Baseball Research since 1979.

CHAPTER 11

North of the Border Again

SEPTEMBER 17, 1994 REUNION OF THE
1951 SCHWAB PEE WEE BASEBALL TEAM
Belleville, Ontario, Canada

After many months of planning, arrangements were finalized for a reunion of the old "51" gang. After receiving a letter from Dick Hurst, the reunion coordinator, confirming the September 17, 1994 date, we (my wife, son Steve, and Pam) packed our bags for the trip to Canada. Dick advised us that the reunion would begin at 2:00 p.m., and last until the lights went out.

We left Harrisburg on September 16th and arrived in Gananague, Ontario, about five hours later. Our stop in Gananague was necessary to contact the former Schwab Pee Wee team catcher, Dave Coe, who lives there. He was unable to attend the reunion because of prior commitments. We talked of the good old days on the diamond in Belleville and about what he and I had been doing over the years. It was nice to see old Davey. He had not changed that much physically and still had that boyish face.

After leaving Davey, we continued our trip to Belleville which is about one and one-half hours from Gananague. When we arrived we called our host, Dick Hurst, and he came immediately to guide us to his house. I rode with him, and on the way I told him we had contacted Dave Coe. Seeing Davey and Dick again was quite emotional.

Upon arrival at Dick's home we were greeted by his wife Judy. She is a wonderful person and made us feel right at home during our two day stay there. After we ate dinner that night, we all sat around reminiscing about that special summer of "51" and how our families had fared over the years. Preparations were also begun for hosting the reunion the next day.

In the early hours of September 17th, Dick and my son Steve policed the beautiful grounds surrounding Dick's backyard. They put up lights, including some placed on a large evergreen, and then they cleared the swimming pool of debris. After breakfast Dick took Steve and me on a two-hour tour of Belleville and some of the surrounding towns. Along the way, we picked up the food supplies to be served at the reunion. I was very surprised to see how Belleville had changed over the years. New buildings were evident everywhere. Our visit to the fairgrounds where the Redmen used to play brought back fond memories. Dick showed us some of the buildings that he was instrumental in having built. His position as Chairperson of the Parks Committee afforded him the opportunity to participate in such undertakings.

The Reunion

First to arrive was the team sponsor Ted Schwab and his son, Steve. We embraced and began discussing that special summer of "51". He inquired if I had a picture of the team, and when I told him that I didn't, he handed me a large picture of the team that he had in his possession for the past 43 years. Passing that picture on to me was a class act on his part. I reluctantly accepted it knowing that it was one of his prized possessions. He insisted that I take it back home, and that is exactly where the picture is now. I have it in the family room in my home as a constant reminder of my good old days in Belleville in "51" with my Canadian friends. Mr. Schwab advised me that one of our players, Norm Rushlowe, had passed away and another, Arnold Barclay, had serious health problems. Tommy Cathcart, our assistant coach, couldn't attend because of a death in his family. However, all the other players were scheduled to come, and come they did, one after another. After all the embracing, hugging, and shaking of hands had ended, we settled down to discuss the summer of "51" and our official team photo that Ted had given me.

Ted remarked to me "You know Willie, not one of those lads turned out badly." If in some way I had a part in that and had touched their young hearts along the way, I consider myself lucky.

We took pictures shown in this chapter, and then we said a silent prayer for our departed third baseman, Norm.

After dining on beef kabobs prepared by the Hursts, we continued into the night, thoughtfully remembering our long enduring friendship. As mentioned earlier, this was a special group of individuals. God above must have been smiling to see that his ebony and ivory creations were doing what he intended us to do - love one another.

As I told them, even though I didn't return to coach the team again, I had never forgotten them, their love, friendship, and kindness that were so important to me. I don't know of many organizations that would reunite after 43 years and still have the same spirit of friendship that existed back in "51". You could sense that each of us enjoyed our companionship. Yeah, God above was definitely smiling.

We consumed two cakes. One read "Welcome Back Willie" and the other showed a player sliding into home plate with the catcher and umpire standing close by. One of my players commented, referring to the sliding player on the cake, "Shake it off!"

We agreed that we would try to meet again in Harrisburg in 1995. Mr. Schwab said he would hire a bus and bring the players and their wives to Harrisburg for a visit. Unfortunately, due to everyone's schedules and commitments, we were unable to get together.

During our visit to Canada for the reunion, we were also able to visit the Halls. I lived in their home in 1951 during my playing days with the Redmen. They are up in age now but remain alert and remember many of the good times we enjoyed.

The reunion was fantastic. To be able to see people you haven't seen in 43 years, but who had remained friends, was simply amazing. It was the thrill of a lifetime. My young Canadian friends had grown to be fine, outstanding, and successful men, and I am extremely proud of them. As Mr. Schwab so eloquently stated, "This reunion was one in a million." I couldn't agree more.

On the return trip home my wife commented "something special happened in 1951 to create such a bond of friendship" between my players and me. What happened was a special group of young Canadians accepted me and gave me the name of "Willie", which was their sign of affection for me. It has been a blessing and joy to be associated with them both on and off the diamond. I guess the shy lad from Millerstown and Newport had fulfilled part of his boyhood dream by being able to coach and be affiliated with such wonderful individuals as my Canadian friends on the 1951 Schwab Pee Wee baseball team.

The photos of the reunion on the next few pages capture only the surface of an event that was a highlight of my life. My son videotaped the proceedings so my family can recapture the get-together at our leisure.

REUNION

1951 SCHWABS PEEWEE BASEBALL TEAM
and SPOUSES

SATURDAY, SEPT. 17, 1994

2:PM until the Lights go out

SPECIAL GUESTS:

COACH WILLIE FORDHAM
and MRS.FORDHAM

at HURST'S HOME 9 VINE CRESC.

BELLEVILLE, ONTARIO

Please bring lawn chairs, bathing suits and towels, ball gloves and BYOB.

Please plan to attend this special reunion. Willy is really looking forward to seeing you all again.

HOSTS: DICK and JUDY HURST

RSVP: 613 962-9874

Ted and I with the team members' wives at the September 17, 1994 Reunion in Belleville, Ontario, Canada

Schwab's won peewee baseball title in 1951

Recalling the Glory Days

"Recalling the Glory Days"
article written by Mr. Paul Svoboda
(The Intelligencer *newspaper, 1995)*

By Paul Svoboda
The Intelligencer

It's a summer that Willie Fordham will never forget.

Over 40 years later, his voice fills with emotion as he remembers two months in 1951 in Belleville and a gang of apple-cheeked boys eager to learn about baseball and life.

"It was a wonderful summer," said Fordham in a recent telephone interview from his home in Harrisburg, Pennsylvania. "I'll never forget those little kids."

Those 'little kids' are now grown men with families, successful careers and their own fond memories of an unforgettable summer of baseball and good times.

"Willie Fordham was a man who gave us guidance, inspiration and hope," says Dick Hurst, a member of that 1951 Schwab's peewee baseball team.

Last summer, Hurst organized the first reunion of the Schwab's team. The team was among four in the first-ever organized youth baseball league in Belleville.

"They were a losing team until I took over," said Fordham. "I'm not bragging or anything. I just tried to teach them to be good men.

"Mr. Schwab (team sponsor Ted Schwab) told me not one of them turned out bad."

The players, as they'll tell you today, formed an immediate bond with Fordham. A special bond, Hurst insists.

"He was a respected teacher," he says. "A coach. A friend."

With Fordham's help, the Schwab's team went on to win the league championship.

"They did everything I asked them to do," says Fordham.

And sometimes more. The team held practices every weekday morning at 9 a.m. but Fordham remembers differently.

"Every morning at 6 a.m. I'd hear this big noise outside my window," he laughed. "It was the kids. They'd say, 'Come on Willie, let's play ball.' They'd practice from dawn to dusk."

As far as Hurst and his baseball-playing buddies were concerned, the road that brought a 23-year-old black American baseball coach to a small Ontario town in 1951 was simply one of good fortune for them. But it was Fordham's skill as a lefthanded hurler that originally led him to Belleville.

A native of Carlisle, Pennsylvania, Fordham pitched college baseball and eventually ended up playing for pay in a league out of Philadelphia. A U.S. scout, bird-dogging for the Oshawa Merchants, offered the southpaw an opportunity to join the Motor City outfit and Fordham headed north. From the Merchants, he joined the Belleville Redmen for the 1951 season.

Fordham boarded with Jack Hall and his family and accepted an offer from Schwab to coach the peewees.

"Everybody took me in," said Fordham. "They treated me just like a member of the family. Even though I was black I wasn't shown any prejudice.

"The kids made my summer and the Redmen were all good guys."

After his stint in Belleville, Fordham had a tryout with the old Brooklyn Dodgers and was farmed out to their double-A affiliate in Harrisburg, where he lives today.

But even a shot at cracking a Major League roster didn't leave the same imprint on Fordham's mind as did that 1951 season and the Schwab's boys. And, according to Fordham, last summer's reunion reaffirmed that fact.

"That reunion is something I'll never forget," he said. "I could just see the love and friendship there.

"There aren't too many organizations after 43 years that could come back and have a reunion like that."

So successful was the get-together, in fact, that plans are already in the works for another one next summer. And this time, Fordham is looking forward to playing host.

"Mr. Schwab said he's going to hire a bus and come down to visit us," said Fordham.

It's a good bet Fordham — and his Schwab's boys — can't wait.

The 1951 Schwab Pee Wee Baseball Team

(left to right) Back row: Willie Fordham (coach), Jon Warren, Tom Cathcart, Steve Schwab, John Foster, Norm Rushlowe and Ted Schwab (sponsor). In the middle: Dick Hurst, Bob Alexander, Ron "Bomber" Barclay. In the front: Dave Coe, Jim Meagher and Jack Elliott.

The Schwab boys in 1994

(left to right) Back row: Willie Fordham, Jon Warren, Steve Schwab, John Foster and Ted Schwab. In the middle: Dick Hurst, Bob Alexander and Ron "Bomber" Keller. In front: Jim Meagher and Jack Elliott. Absent: Dave Coe, Arnold "Turk" Barclay, Tom Cathcart and Norm Rushlowe (deceased).

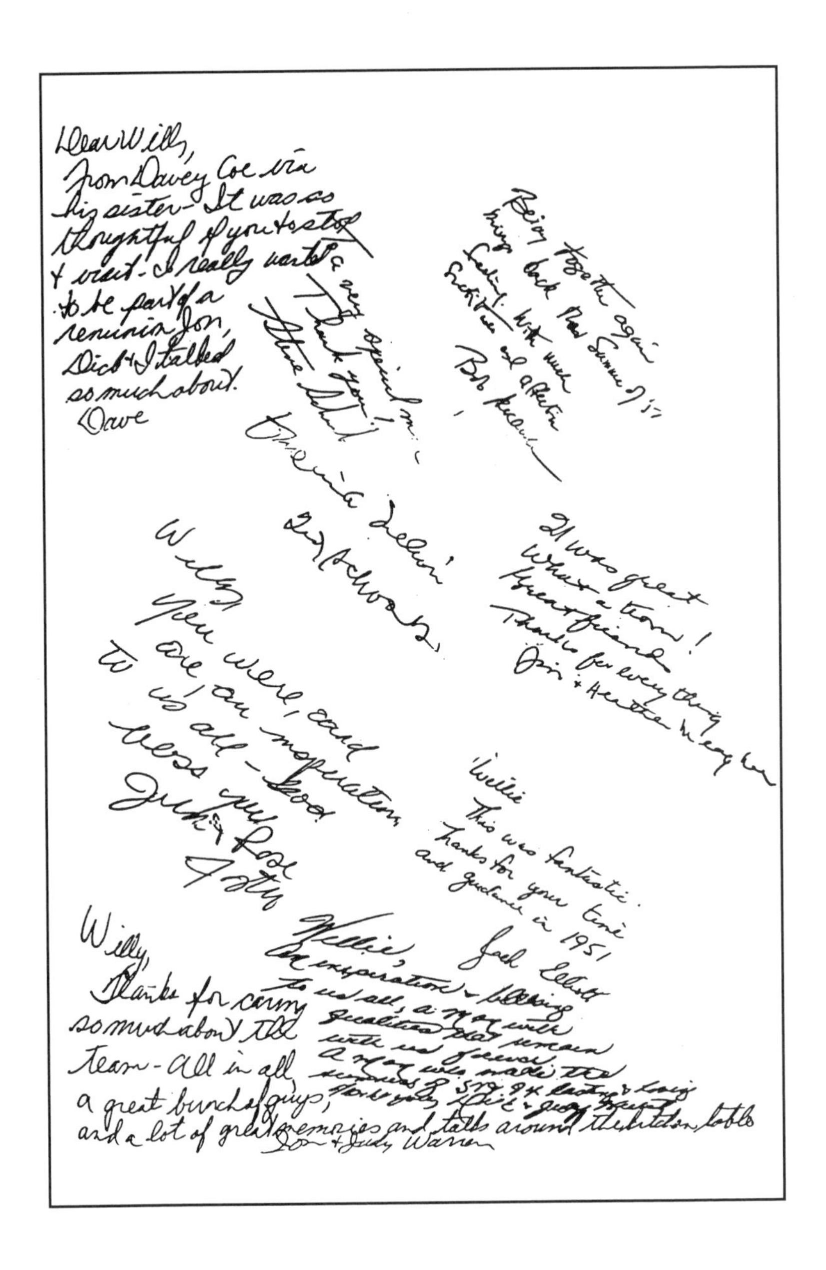

Dear Willy,
From Davey Coe via his sister - It was so thoughtful of you to stop & visit - I really wanted to be part of a reunion Jon, Dick & I talked so much about.
Dave

Willie
This was fantastic.
Thanks for your time and guidance in 1951
Jack Elliott

Willy,
Thanks for caring so much about the team - All in all a great bunch of guys, and a lot of great memories and talks around the kitchen table

Comments written by Schwab Pee Wee baseball team members

Arnold Barclay, our second baseman on the 1951 Schwab Pee Wee baseball team, passed away on January 30, 1995. His brother, Hugh Barclay, prepared a booklet entitled, "In Lieu of Flowers" in memory of his departed brother. An excerpt from Hugh's booklet appears below:

Schwab Baseball Team 1951

Arnold was a member of Schwab's Baseball Team that played in the Belleville Pee Wee league. Ironically, they had a reunion for the team in Belleville just prior to Arn's surgery of September 19, 1994. I was able to establish that Dick Hurst, one of Arn's teammates, had organized the reunion. I contacted Dick to set up a meeting with some of the other players and myself regarding Arn's baseball career. Dick told me that the team had phoned Arn and spoke with him prior to his surgery. After the phone call, the team stood in a circle with hands joined, and said a prayer for Arn and Norm Rushlowe. I had the pleasure to meet with Dick Hurst, Jack Elliott and Tommy Cathcart on May 2nd, 1995. They informed me that Arn had played second base. When I inquired as to the rationale behind the choice of positions, they were quick to point out that Arn's arm wasn't strong enough to throw in from the outfield, or from third to first, so second base seemed to be a logical choice. Furthermore they pointed out that Arn was fearless and didn't mind placing his body in front of a fast moving groundball to get an "out". As a matter of fact, they pointed out that Arn's barrel chest was very appropriate to the task.

The team was made up from kids who attended Queen Alexander Public School and was one of the original teams to make up the first minor league baseball team in the history of Belleville. They practiced every morning from 9:30 to 12:00 noon at the Belleville fairgrounds. The practice was held under the eye of coach Willie Fordham. Willie was an import from Pennsylvania who had been brought to Belleville by the Belleville Redmen as a pitcher. Willie would begin the practice by having the kids run around the race track, and if they were late for practice, they would have to do it twice. Dick and the boys described that summer of 1951 as the best summer of their childhood. Tommy Cathcart could remember who they played their first game against, what the score was, and what he and Jack Elliott had discussed before the game. They said that Arn was a left-handed hitter (What other kind is there?). Arn liked to bunt and was pretty good at beating them out. When I asked if Arn had ever had an altercation with the umpire, they all thought for a few seconds and then agreed that on occasion, Arn would stomp back to the dugout after a called third strike muttering expletives regarding the umpire. On occasion these eruptions continued from the dugout. (Now who would ever had guessed such a thing would take place.)

In reply to a letter I received from Janet (Arn's wife), I wrote the following letter to her on March 18, 1995:

Dear Janet,

My wife and I are very sorry to hear about Arnold's passing. The good Lord must have needed a dedicated husband and a baseball player, so he chose Arnold.

As you stated in your letter, he was a wonderful person. I only knew him for a short span of time, three months during the summer of 1951, but I never forgot him.

He was one of my best players on the team. I could always count on him. You only had to tell him what to do once and he never forgot. Besides being a team player who always gave his best effort, I remember his quiet manner and tremendous drive, even as a twelve year old.

It was a pleasure to hear his voice on the phone when we talked to him at the hospital during the September 1994 reunion at Dick Hurst's house.

Please send us some pictures of your family. Attached are pictures of how the team looked in 1951 and then in 1994. We missed you good folks at the reunion, but we knew our good buddy would have been with us if he could. I know he would have enjoyed seeing the old gang. Turk was one of us and we felt his presence throughout the day as we reminisced about the summer of 1951.

Please keep in touch, and our prayers are with you and your family.

With fondest regards,
Willie

CHAPTER 12

Life Goes On

MY BRUSH WITH DEATH

In early 1982, I was diagnosed as being diabetic. It was no surprise because I had lost weight, was always thirsty, and constantly urinating, all sure signs of diabetes. My mom was diabetic and, being the first of her three children, I may have inherited her condition.

Over the years I have been taking insulin shots daily. As a direct result of my diabetes, my eyesight was affected. In early 1994, major surgery was performed by Dr. Brian Lerner on my left eye at the Mercy Hospital in Baltimore, Maryland. Later in 1994, laser beam treatment was used to seal up leaking blood vessels in my eye. In addition, surgery was performed by Dr. Bennett Chotiner on both eyes to remove cataracts. Diabetes is a disease which causes major damage to the human body. Hopefully, someday they may find a cure for this dreaded disease.

Thanks to my wife Jessie's carefully planned meals, my diabetes has been controlled. To those of you suffering a similar condition, take heed and follow your doctor's advice, and you can live a normal life. The important thing is to watch your diet. Also, get in the habit of walking and other exercise activities.

In June of 1991, I got the shock of my life. I had a major heart attack which caused tremendous damage to my heart muscle. Thanks to the professional help of Dr. Stanley Lewin, my Cardiologist, I was released from the Polyclinic Hospital in Harrisburg eight days after the attack. Having been physically active all my life, reality set in when I was advised by Doctor Lewin that changes in my life-style were necessary. These physical limitations that were imposed were heartbreaking (no pun intended).

No longer could I get out with my lawn mower and mow my lawn. This had been a labor of love, especially seeing how beautiful the lawn appeared after the mowing. No longer could I do the physical tasks required in my T.V. shop. No lifting, no this, and no that! I also had to give up going outside to shovel snow. No longer, as another doctor told me, could I run a mile race. There sure are a lot of NO CAN DO'S!

In spite of the imposed physical limitations, life goes on. Each day when I awaken, I thank the good Lord above for giving me another day. A day that may result in my touching some hearts and helping those in need. I have always believed that life has purpose and meaning, and that things happen for a reason. But it seems as though you have a little voice inside whispering that today could be your last. My advice to everyone with similar conditions is that we be thankful for being alive to:

see the sun rise

hear the birds singing

enjoy enduring family/friends relationships

spread joy throughout your daily traveling

be a friend to someone

In October 1994 I had a serious setback, I found out one evening that I could not breathe. I was rushed to the Polyclinic Hospital in Harrisburg where I had a brush with death. They told me later that while I was in the emergency room, my heart stopped beating. Fortunately, using those electric-shock paddles, they were able to get my heart beating again. After a two-week stay in the hospital, I was sent home to recuperate. A battery of pills were prescribed, which I take daily. Again, I am thankful to be alive in spite of my physical limitations. Apparently, my work here on earth is not finished.

Everyone asked how I felt when my heart stopped beating, and if I saw that tunnel of light that you are supposed to see when you pass over. In reply, all I could say was that everything was peaceful; however, I didn't see that tunnel of light.

The brush with death has significantly altered my views. I am more observant of my surroundings and people. I also now realize that the facade can be very deceiving. A smile may mask the hurt inside, and unfortunately, kindness may be interpreted as a sign of weakness.

So to all of you who have suffered a malady similar to mine, take heed and live each day to the fullest, **always thanking the good Lord above for His blessings.**

CHAPTER 13

How Beautiful They Are... My Family Members

As explained earlier, my dad and mom separated shortly after I was born. Regretfully, I never got the chance to know my dad, to find out if I liked him, or if he would have liked me. Would he have taken me fishing, boating, and so forth? He has passed this life, but I had always hoped that he would have been proud of me. Mom said he was an accomplished auto mechanic. Too bad I didn't get the chance to pal around with him, not only as his son but as his friend.

I was fortunate to have my grandfather to take the place of my dad. I truly loved and needed Pop. Being in his presence made me realize that he was a wonderful human being that was blessed with God-given powers. He passed away many years ago, but the quality times we spent together are remembered. I will always be grateful for his caring ways and sense of values that he honed into me.

Even though my siblings and I do not see each other on a daily basis, we stay in touch. As I mentioned previously, they are only a phone call away. Throughout our lives, we were taught by our elders to love one another. This, I can truthfully say, we have done. Each of us knows that the other two will be there if needed. It really is a blessing to have grown up with two people for whom you continue to have a great deal of love and admiration. They are and always will be my loved ones.

My stepfather, Loomis Edwards, is in his nineties, but he is in relatively good health. He has always been a good provider and sadly misses my mom. They had good times together. He provided a nice home for mom and made sure she was happy and content. His favorite expression is "Let's book!" which means it is time to go. He lives in Carlisle with my sister, Mary. His relatives reside in Raleigh, North Carolina.

In December of 1955, I married my wife Jessie. We have been married over forty years and have three sons, Stephen (Casper), Daniel (Putt), and Byron (Monk). Each has his own pleasing personality. The sense of values taught to me by my grandfather were passed to our sons from the time they were born. I can truthfully say they have grown up to be fine men with many outstanding qualities.

Even though the quality time spent with them was limited because of my two jobs, I have gained their respect over the years. They are always doing so many nice things for me and their mother. Their nicknames came about as follows:

Son Steve: I nicknamed him Casper or simply Cass. Steve is a telecommunications specialist and is considered a computer mainframe expert. He has several children and grandchildren. He also worked at the depot for a number of years and received many awards for his outstanding performance. He currently works for a financial corporation.

Son Daniel: He was always the one to forget to put things back where they belonged, so I nicknamed him Putt.

Dan is a gifted musician. He has written many original songs, has recorded several albums, and is recognized as one of the top musicians in the area. Daniel also has performed major roles in plays at a theater in Harrisburg. He has five children and his wife is the former Shelmar Johnson.

Son Byron: I explained to him that the monks of old were very wise and intelligent people. So I nicknamed him Monk. Byron lives in Maryland and is a Systems Analyst for a defense contractor. He is also a gifted musician. He served in the U.S. Navy for over eight years immediately after graduation from high school in 1977. He graduated (with honors) from the University of Maryland in December 1994 and is currently working on his Master's degree at Maryland. He has one daughter.

Jessie, my wife and mother of our three sons, was a Language Arts teacher in the Harrisburg School District. She has been a pillar of strength keeping the good ship "FORDHAM" on a steady course. She is not only my wife but my best friend.

She recently retired as a school teacher in the Harrisburg School District (June 1996). She is also an honor graduate of Penn State University (1984). She is an excellent cook and a very neat housekeeper. Thanks to her, I always have nice clothes to wear. Like most couples, we had our conflicts, but overall we have had many good times together.

Jessie, the boys and I enjoyed traveling. Our many trips to Canada were exciting. We also would go on sled rides in the winter. The boys enjoyed the swimming pool that my brother-in-law, James Fountain Jr., and I put in our Calder Street backyard. That project lasted about six months. My wife and I always made sure they enjoyed their home; got enough to eat; attended church; and most importantly to us, stayed healthy. They have children of their own now and have tried to be good fathers. I am very proud of their efforts.

Mood swings of parents can seriously affect behavior

patterns of their children. In my estimation, this may be a major problem in many households. The father who has struggled to realize his full potential may unknowingly shift moods daily without any thought of how it could disrupt the harmonious relationships of his family members.

The black man is constantly attempting to prove not only to himself, but to humanity as a whole, that he is in fact a man. A man blessed with God-given talents. History points out that black men have made significant contributions to the world community in many fields of endeavor. I only hope that my contributions to my family were worthwhile.

My Extended Family Members

My wife, Jessie, has three sisters and a brother who reside in Harrisburg. The oldest sister, Marjorie ("Marge"), graduated from East Los Angeles Junior College for Nursing. After graduation, she was employed as a nurse (LPN) at the Los Angeles County General Hospital for six years. She moved to Stamford, Connecticut where, from 1960 to 1965, she was employed as a nurse at the Stamford Hospital. In 1982 we packed up Marge's belongings and brought her to Harrisburg. Marge had been my good buddy. She passed away in 1998.

Judith, the next to the oldest, has two children, Jeffrey and J. Michelle, and a granddaughter (Jeffrey's daughter) named Ashleigh. Judith was the first black woman to serve on Harrisburg's City Council. Jeff graduated from Northeastern University located in Boston, Massachusetts and currently resides in Harrisburg. Michelle graduated from the Rhode Island School of Design located in Providence, Rhode Island, where she earned a Bachelor of Fine Arts (BFA) degree. She also graduated from Howard University in Washington, DC. Michelle and her husband, Jimmy, live in New York City. She has traveled extensively working and teaching in the textile industry. She has taught textile courses in such far away places as Zimbabwe, Nigeria, and Sierra Leone in Africa. Judith makes an imperial crab meat salad that is out of this world! I've always been very close to her and her children.

Georgia, is a retired social worker and lives in Harrisburg. She has two children, Rhonda and Ronald, and a granddaughter. Her husband (now deceased), William "Bill" Mays, was Harrisburg's first black Police Captain. During one Christmas season, Georgia and I were partners in a Christmas tree selling operation that was able to make a small profit. I always enjoyed spending time with all of the Mays family members.

James "Jamie", is the only brother and is married to the former Lauree Middleton from Steelton, PA. They have four sons (and daughter-in-laws), James (Levern), Mike (Tamu), Roger (Loridonna), Larry (Tracy), and several grandchildren. James, a Real Estate salesperson, is retired from the Mechanicsburg Naval Supply Depot. As I mentioned earlier, he was extremely helpful in getting a swimming pool ready that I was building for my sons at our home on Calder Street. He also helped me do some grounds work at a place near Harrisburg called Seven Stars, where I had planned to build a cabin. All of the family would gather at our house for Thanksgiving and at James and Lauree's house on Christmas evening for good food and fun. At these family gatherings, James, Bill Mays, and I would sing our own version of the "Battle Hymn of the Republic," much to the delight of the family. We've shared many special times with James and his family.

Taking my nephews and niece, Michelle, to and from the New England colleges they were attending was an annual ritual. We would load up my van and take off. Fortunately, we had no mishaps or mechanical failures. Now that they have graduated, I sort of miss the trips and fun times. They were always anxious to return to school but were also happy to return home.

Cousins Leon and Jackie Green

My cousin Leon, Uncle Ed's son, and his wife Jackie remain in touch. They have recently moved into a beautiful new home they had built in Harrisburg. Leon is a gifted handyman. He lived in Carlisle with my mom for many years and excelled in track events. He and I are the "experts" in planning our annual family reunions. He has several children and grandchildren, two sisters, Beverly and Rhonda, and a brother, Jim.

CHAPTER 14

Friends

Mom always told me to hold on to dear, true friends and don't let go; they are more precious than gold. The following are friends who have enriched my life and have been an invaluable source of joy and pleasure. As mom instructed me, these are friends that I will hold onto and never let go. I would like to introduce them. Those with an * have passed this life.

Gladys Burns

I met Gladys while working at the Mechanicsburg depot and our friendship has lasted over thirty-five years. She has two daughters, Sharon and Tori. Tori and her husband Robert reside in California. My wife and I are also her god-parents. She is a sweet person and continually sends us very nice presents. Sharon has two sons, Jason and Tony. All call me "Uncle Bill". Gladys is very active in her church and community. She sings in the choir and has a beautiful voice. I can remember all those goodies she would bring to my shop to tide me over until I got home. I will never forget the good times going to and from work at the depot. I can truly say that Gladys is a princess, one of a kind, and a superstar, but most importantly, a true friend.

Charley (Sleepy) Davis

Charley ran a pool room on Sixth Street in Harrisburg. Many fellows from all walks of life (teachers, laborers, state workers, etc) visited the pool room, primarily because Charley made everyone feel so welcome. Each day there was furious action on the pool tables, but he made sure that everything remained in order. There was no cussing, fighting, or other indignities allowed.

To me Charley was a friend; one who provided a place where you could kick back and really enjoy yourself at the tables. I can remember a time when I lost about $40.00 at the tables. As I was leaving, he handed me a twenty dollar bill, knowing I was dead broke. He never asked for the return of the twenty, but I suppose he got that twenty back many times over the years, plus a lot more since I was a frequent guest at his pool room.

Charley was one of those guys who would give you the shirt off his back if you needed it. He was a big, robust man with a hearty laugh that made his belly jump up and down like jelly. At the pool room, I met a lot of fellows who found Charley's place to be a relief from the daily work grind where matters of importance could be discussed.

The pool room is no longer there and Charley has passed this life, but he left a ton of memories behind.

Sidney DeKnight

Sidney was a classmate at Cheyney University and was always the gentleman and well-groomed. Also, he was an accomplished musician and played the organ in many churches in the Philadelphia area. During the summer months, on breaks from classroom studies, Sidney would invite me to stay at his home with his parents. They treated me like one of their own, and for that, I will always be grateful.

Sidney's gone but will never be forgotten. Rest in peace dear friend.

Charles Hall

Another friend and neighbor who I met working at the Mechanicsburg Depot is Charles Hall. He would ride with Jessie and me to and from the depot. He is married to the former Charlene Douglas. They have two daughters, Debbie and Dawn. Their son, Doug, passed away at a very young age. Charlene was a Special Education teacher and a Home Economics teacher in York. Every year Charles would visit us for several hours at our home on Calder Street on Christmas day, helping my young chargers enjoy their gifts. He especially helped with the bikes which, at their young ages, were difficult to maneuver. His children and our sons enjoyed each other's company. He coached my son Byron's little league baseball team. Charles was always nice to be around because of his pleasing personality and charm. We don't see each other much now, but when we do, it is a constant reminder of those good old days spent on Calder Street.

Marlin Hicks

Marlin Hicks is a friend I worked with in the Planning Division at Mechanicsburg. His wife, Myrtle, graduated from my alma mater, Cheyney, and his son is a lawyer with a prestigious firm in Washington, DC. Marlin and I were the first black members of the Federal Credit Union Credit Committee at SPCC. He was later elevated to the Board of Directors, a position he held for many years. From time to time we would discuss how some people viewed the affairs of our ethnic group, and one distinct phrase came to mind: Persona Non Grata (invisible, unwanted). As members of the credit committee, we were determined to ensure that all people were treated fairly and equally. Marlin is also an accomplished chef and specializes in seafood salads. I clearly remember the time he brought his delicious crab meat salad to my shop. My helper, Reggie, wanted some but he was sternly warned by Marlin that the salad was for my consumption, and he could have some if I wanted to share with him. Needless to say, he was able to enjoy the salad along with me. Marlin and I remain in touch and update each other concerning our family happenings.

Dick and Judy Hurst
(Belleville, Ontario, Canada)

Dick was captain of the 1951 Schwab Pee Wee baseball team and has kept in touch over the years. He and wife, Judy, took time out on 17 September 1994 to host a reunion of the team. I will never forget their kindness to me and my family.

Lois Maloney

Lois has been a family friend for many years. She and my wife were raised in the same neighborhood and attended the same schools. She has two sons named Clark and Greg. She has a powerful singing voice and is also a graduate of Cheyney University.

****James (Bud) Oakley***

Bud was a classmate at Carlisle High School and a neighbor down the street. He was a constant companion, and we were always going to the nearby towns to search for girlfriends; and we had many. We also stood our ground when the bullies in Carlisle tried to shove us around. Luckily, we both knew how to fight, so we didn't lose any of those battles.

I was best man at his wedding which was a very memorable occasion. He would always invite me to his home to watch the Friday night fights. At these gatherings, his mother would prepare delicious food for us to eat. In return for his kindness and friendship, he would always be allowed to ride in the good old Ford. Isn't that what being friends is all about?

My friend Bud is gone, but he was a big part of my life during my teenage years; he was like a brother to me. Bud was my true and loyal friend and will never be forgotten.

Julius Reeves

Julius Reeves has been one of my closest friends for many years. He has been a patient at the Lebanon VA Medical Center for the past three years. He is married to the former Jane Davis. They have two daughters, Chrissy and Allison, and a son named Justin. Julius is a retired Middletown (PA) School District school teacher. He was a very active referee in numerous athletic contests. We attended many horse racing events in the local and surrounding areas. He is a skilled handicapper. One particular night at the local race track, he won a race worth a considerable amount of money. Being his old buddy, he shared some of his winnings with me. Julius can no longer run up and down the court as he once did, but his spirits remain upbeat and he continues to flash his beautiful smile.

Leroy Shirk ("Taxi")

At an early age Taxi began working with me on my trash collecting business. He was up early each morning eager to begin work and was very helpful loading and unloading items we picked up. When I left Carlisle, I didn't see Taxi for many years, but we have met occasionally over recent years to discuss the good old days. He is still the same Taxi I knew back in the early 50s but is much wiser. I will never forget my good friend.

Lewis Watson

Lewis is a friend I also met while working at Mechanicsburg. He is a certified Public Accountant (CPA) and has prepared my income tax returns for the past 40 years. He is a classic example of what friendship is all about. He has health problems similar to mine, but these problems have not diminished his zest for life.

Schwab Pee Wee Baseball Team Members

They made the summer of 1951 special. It was great fun coaching them and taking part in the many get togethers after the games ended. They are listed below:

Bob Alexander
Dave Coe
John Foster
Jim Meagher
Steve Schwab
Asst. Coach - Tommy Cathcart
*Arnold Barclay
Jack Elliott
Dick Hurst
*Norm Rushlowe
Jon Warren
Sponsor -Ted Schwab

John and Nancy Talley

John and Nancy Talley have been good friends for many years. They have two daughters, Joline and Joan (who is deceased), and a son named John. They have always been there when needed. We get together often and talk about the good old days. My wife and Nancy are just like sisters. They share many things in common; both deeply love God and family and are actively involved in life.

CHAPTER 15

In their own words...

My Family's Comments

In this chapter, I share some comments and thoughts from my wife Jessie, and sons Stephen, Daniel, and Byron. As explained earlier, even though I worked two jobs for the majority of the time I have been married and may not have been able to spend as much time with my family as I would have liked, we have always had love, God's blessings, and a strong family bond that continues to keep us together.

My Wife Jessie's Comments

It has been fascinating for me to watch my husband, Wilbur, recuperate from congestive heart failure, because it has progressed along with this book. He began writing his autobiography when he was a patient in the Polyclinic Medical Center, and he has worked on it daily for over two years.

As his health improved, he worked longer hours on his book.

His enthusiasm for "the project", as he and I affectionately named it, never faded from start to finish. Wilbur was always anxious to talk to anyone, anytime and anywhere, about his work-in-progress.

What began as a therapeutic adventure has ended as an accomplished labor of love. "The project" has especially touched the lives of our sons and me, because we have witnessed first-hand the good it has done for someone very precious to us.

Neither a complainer nor a quitter, Wilbur was not about to let his illness stop him. So, when the challenge presented itself, God gave him the strength he needed to put forth the effort it took to accomplish his goals.

He survived heart failure and completed this book, and we are all very grateful to God for his blessings. Once again, Wilbur proved that he is a determined man who insisted on giving whatever he does "his best shot." I am extremely proud of him and his efforts. Love you Big Guy!

My Son Steve's Comments

They call him "Will", "Bill", "Willie", "Teach", "Wilbur", "Grandad", "Hap", and "Mr. Greenford", but I call him "Dad". Do I call him Dad because of the time he took to try to show my brothers and me respect for life? I think so. Do I call him Dad because he took the time to involve me in his television business at the mere age of 5 years old, teaching me the business? I think so. Do I call him Dad because of his uncompromising and unconditional love for my mother, brothers, the entire family, and me? I think so. In fact, reader, I know so!

This book only tells part of the history of a man who was born during the Great Depression, raised in a small town, lost his father before he was a teenager, put himself through college, was invited and participated in the Brooklyn Dodger training camp, served his country during World War II, nurtured our family of five, and to date, continues to share his knowledge and love to all he surveys. I am blessed to have been the son of a man of such intelligence, devotion, love of life, and compassion to give a stranger the shirt off his back if the stranger was in need.

Growing up in his castle as the oldest of three sons, I didn't always meet my dad's standards or expectations, nor did I always follow his rules. However, I did, thank God, remember his words of wisdom and the character imprint he placed in me, because if I hadn't, I would not be able to place these words of text into this book today. As with most young males of any species, I challenged Dad while I was a teenage male, and quickly learned and remembered one of Dad's most famous quotes, "Don't try to build yourself through illusions of grandeur." The incident was short lived but created a rift between my Dad and me for years.

It took quite some time before I found out the value of his unconditional, uncompromising love. As with a pride of lions, the young male attempts to assert his youthful ways towards the Alpha male, and the wiser and stronger Alpha male must vanquish him from the pride. During my absence, I utilized all the tools, wisdom, and courage Dad gave me to survive, and survive I did. Now he and I are best friends, and partners in the same television business he started over 35 years ago.

As you, the reader, absorbed the text, hopefully you have realized as I have that "Will", "Bill", "Willie", "Teach", "Wilbur", "Grandad", "Hap", and "Mr. Greenford" not only has, does, and is very capable of wearing all those hats, he is bigger than all those hats combined. He is my father, and next to God Almighty you don't get much bigger than that. I LOVE YOU DAD!

–Stephen Blaine "Casper" Fordham

My Son Daniel's Comments

Growing up in the FORDHAM house was a wonderful experience, and one that, if I could, I would not change. Like any family we had our good and our bad times, but the thing that stuck with me is that I never heard my dad say a cuss word. I never heard of him doing drugs, and I never saw him abuse my mom. I never heard of my dad cheating on my mom. My dad was probably then, and still is now, the model father. I wish that I would have had more time with him to study the things that he knew and learned in his life, like baseball, electronics, how to speak to people, etc... I used to always put my dad in the same category as Muhammad Ali because he has the same courage and perseverance as the champ. I never saw my dad afraid of anything. I remember certain things that I will point out so you can see how I saw my dad, Wilbur Fordham.

When I was very young I had a creative imagination and I would see things in my room that I could have sworn were creatures in the night. I remember plenty of nights when my dad would come into the room and sleep with me so I could get to sleep. I would look at my dad's giant back and feel safe for the night, until the next night or two when I would call him in again. I also remember dad taking us out back and making us his baseball catchers. I remember the baseball always slipping off the top of my glove and hitting me in the face. I would always cry and dad would just say "Shake it off boy." Needless to say that after a few of those, I hung up my baseball career. My younger brother followed in those footsteps a little further than I did. As a matter of fact, it got to the point where I couldn't walk by a baseball field without getting hit by the ball.

I also remember the Christmases that we had. I felt that my dad thought I was special to him. I felt like he was my best friend in all the world because on Christmas it seemed like I always had more gifts than my brothers. Then, as I got older, I realized that it was probably because I almost died of appendicitis when I was young, and I think dad was just saying "thank you Lord for not taking my boy away." Well, once his thanks wore off, I was treated like the other sons that I knew Dad loved also. The gravy train ride was over, and I found out that my best friend had other best friends. Believe it or not, I was very traumatized by that revelation, but I grew out of it in time.

My dad worked two jobs to keep us fed and happy, so I never saw him as much as I would have liked. I saw him every day from 4:30 pm to 6:00 pm weekdays and then on Sundays. When he was home there was always something going on. Dad was the life of the party, a very family type person. We would have family reunions and get-togethers, and I think that Dad maybe looked at us like we were his team. He always tried to keep family functions going on, with the help of my equally caring mother.

Mom and Dad gave us the best teenage life we could have had. My only regret in life is that I wanted to make my dad's dream come true through me. I became a musician and I truly believe that I carried the dream and desires of my dad on my shoulders. I still believe that his dream will come true.

One thing I learned through my life, and sharing those

days that were so precious to me with my family, is that "It's not whether you win or lose, but how you play the game." I LOVE YOU DAD!

–Daniel Lamont "Putt" Fordham

My Son Byron's Comments

I was truly blessed to be able to grow up in the FORDHAM household. I often give thanks to God for blessing me with wonderful parents and brothers whom I love dearly, and I feel love me also. While life hasn't always been easy for us, we always loved, trusted, and believed in God and one another. My dad has always been my hero and my best friend. From the time when I was young, my dad and I seemed to connect with a special bond. When I was old enough to understand the concept of work, I also understood that my dad had a work ethic that I admired. He would leave for his job at Mechanicsburg before dawn, come home at 4:30 pm, eat dinner with the family, take a short nap, then go to his television business until late in the evening. There were many days when I could see in my dad's eyes and face that he didn't feel like going to his shop in the evenings, but he did it anyway, and I knew that he and my mom sacrificed for our family's comfort and well-being.

Even though my dad spent a lot of time at work, his presence was always felt. Discipline, respect for ourselves, and being respectful of others, were just a few of the many tools that my dad and mom provided to my brothers and me that have helped me deal with life's trials and tribulations.

My dad was kind of strict, yet he was fair. They also taught us a sense of community and compassion for others. The limited time that my dad had off from work, he would always find time to take us places and do different things, even though I'm sure he preferred, and needed, rest. He also wouldn't mind if our friends from the neighborhood came along, or just hung out with us. When they were in his house or with him, my dad treated them as one of his own. Discipline and all.

Growing up, my dad was not one to show a lot of outward affection, but there was no question of his unconditional love. He was the type of person that would hold you tight to give you a hug while telling you with a smile on his face, "Get away, I don't want any of that stuff!" He would also take the time every night to come into my room and wake me out of sleep to talk. In the morning he would come into my room and slap my chest to wake me up, just to get me going before he left for work. It was a bit irritating, but I would look forward to getting my sleep interrupted, just so I could see my dad's smiling face.

On more than one occasion, my dad would let me go to the racetrack with him and his friends. Back in the day, the closest track was Charles Town, WV, which was two hours away from Harrisburg. When I would be with them, they would talk to me and provide me with a lot of wisdom. They (especially my dad) would also challenge me to not just take things for face value but to think things through. Even though at times it may have seemed that I wasn't listening to what was being said, in actuality, I took in everything. Occasionally (as long as my homework was completed), I would go to Charles Town with him on a school night, and at the time it was great to have a dad that would let me do something like that. It taught me two things about my dad. First, he spent so much time working, he would (probably against his own better judgment) allow me to be out with him late on a school night just so we could be together. Second, he was preparing me for being responsible for my actions. Whenever I would go with him, with much enthusiasm and often getting back late, I had better be just as enthusiastic about getting up for school the next morning. I didn't mind losing sleep because just being able to be with my dad gave me an energy that is hard to describe, and it still happens whenever I see him now.

My dad is strong, caring, wise, and very giving. Growing up, he always let me be a kid, while all the time, preparing me to be a man. I love him with all my heart and soul.

–Byron Lewis "Monk" Fordham

Appendix A

Reflections

Looking back over my life I considered myself well blessed. Growing up in the small hamlets of Millerstown and Newport with my beloved family members, I developed a solid sense of values which I have adhered to over the years. Later on, during my teenage years in Carlisle, I was able to develop a good work ethic that has sustained me throughout my life. Pitching the no-hit baseball game for Carlisle High School was a major accomplishment of which I am very proud. My tour with Uncle Sam's Army provided me with a keen sense of what this great country is all about.

My four years at Cheyney were well spent, and I am extremely proud of the B.S. degree I earned and the opportunity to join a fraternity of my choice (AϕA).

My visit to Canada to play professional baseball in the summer of 1951 resulted in a friendship with the Schwab Pee Wee baseball team members that has lasted over 44 years, and it has been one of the highlights of my life. Never in my life had I allowed anyone, other than my family, to get as close to me as my Canadian friends. The fond memories of the days long gone by, when I was coaching them on the ball field, remind me that they are a special group of young men. I really enjoyed the pleasure of their company and realize that their acceptance of me was apparently based upon my ability to lead them.

The team sponsor provided all the equipment we needed to play ball. He and their parents were totally supportive of the team and attended all the games. When I entered Dick Hurst's home to attend their farewell party for me that summer, the first thing I heard was their voices shouting in unison "Willie", "Willie", "Willie", ... It doesn't get any better than that, and for that grand moment, they made me feel as though I was the king of the hill. They are a class act and I will never forget them.

My tryout in early 1952 with the Brooklyn Dodgers of the National Baseball League allowed me to see first-hand the abilities needed to become a major league baseball player. The tryout was a major highlight of my professional baseball career. Even though my baseball career ended at the Class AA level with the Harrisburg Senators of the Eastern League, my enthusiasm for the game has never waned. It is truly a game of champions.

My job at the former Mechanicsburg Naval Supply Depot provided my family with financial security and the opportunity to participate in important matters relating to U.S. Naval operations.

Greenford TV has been one of the joys of my life. To have served the greater Harrisburg community for over 35 years has been very satisfying.

Getting married was another highlight. The marriage to Jessie has lasted over forty-four years. There are fond memories of family outings with many of our friends in attendance. It has been most gratifying to know that my family is always there when needed.

My brush with death has made me fully realize that life is precious and meaningful.

Numerous kudos have been received in recognition of my "giving it my best shot." One of great significance was Harrisburg Mayor Reed's designation of July 15, 1994 as "Wilbur Lewis Fordham Day" in the city of Harrisburg. On that day I was the center of attraction. Maybe, just maybe, this lad from the small hamlets of Millerstown and Newport made some contributions to society that resulted in those kind words of appreciation.

In the final analysis I realize that:
Many have crossed my path along the way,
Some I vividly remember each passing day,
For those soon forgotten,
I wonder why in my memory bank they did not stay,
But if those forgotten reappear,
I wish they'd remain among those daily remembered,
And will not again stray...

What the future holds remains a mystery. I have been truly blessed knowing my family is there when needed. I have never forgotten the days when that old horsehide was being thrown at great velocity through the tire hanging on my grandfather's garage, making my dreams of playing professional baseball a reality. "I gave it my best shot" at stardom and that is all that matters. Yeah, the shy lad from the small hamlets of Millerstown and Newport has been truly blessed, and to be alive after the heart failure is certainly a gift from God above.

APPENDIX B: INDEX